THE
FIRE
OF
PEACE

A PRAYER BOOK

Compiled and edited by
Mary Lou Kownacki, OSB

Table of Contents

INTRODUCTION

PRAYERS FOR LIFE'S JOURNEY
    Peace and Guidance   3
    Family Prayers   17
    Prayers of Concern   24
    Prayers of Praise   42
    Special People, Special Events   52

DAILY PRAYERS FOR ORDINARY TIME
    Daily Morning and Evening   77
    Midday   112
    Night   114

PRAYING THROUGH THE YEAR
    Advent   119
    Christmas   122
    Lent   127
    Easter   131

MARY, WELLSPRING OF PEACE
    Prayers   139
    Litanies   148
    Rosary   154

LITANIES   169

VOWS, PLEDGES and CREEDS   187

STATIONS OF THE CROSS   199

FASTING   213

EXAMINATION OF CONSCIENCE   221

MEDITATIVE PRAYER   233

READINGS FOR THE JOURNEY
    Non-scriptural   243
    Scriptural   263

ACKNOWLEDGEMENTS   285

Introduction

To pick up a prayerbook
is more dangerous than throwing a torch
into a dry woodland.

In a burning forest you can run for cover,
but if you begin to pray
there is no escape,
no place you can hide
from the raging fire of God.

At least that's what happened to the saints
when they prayed.
All of them will testify
that their encounter with God
was like gold being tested in a furnace,
seven times refined.

Saint Teresa of Avila warns:
"authentic prayer
changes us—unmasks us—strips us. . . ."

What she means, I think,
is that sitting in the presence of a passionate
God purges away all the dross, all the impurities
of selfishness, pride, falsehood, hypocrisy,
meanness until only pure gold remains.

It's no wonder, then, that many kneel
just outside the furnace door —
close enough to keep warm,
far enough to keep from getting consumed —
and call it prayer.
Certainly this is a comforting and consoling
exercise, but it is not prayer.

The ancient desert elders said it this way:
"Abba Lot went to see Abba Joseph and said,
'Abba, as much as I am able
I practice a small rule, all the little fasts,
some prayer and meditation, remain quiet,
and as much as possible I keep my thoughts
clean.
What else should I do?
Then the old man stood up
and stretched out his hands toward heaven,
and his fingers became like torches of flame.
And he said, "If you wish, you can be turned into
fire."

And there's the crux: "Do you wish?"
Do you wish to be turned into fire?

By picking up this prayerbook
you have already stepped into the furnace.
But to melt into pure gold
you must hold fast
as the temperature inside continues to rise.

To be turned into fire, you must believe
that if you knock, God will answer.

To be turned into fire,
you must move toward a forgiving heart,
working through any legitimate anger
against those who have hurt or harmed you.

To be turned into fire,
you must be patient and persistent,
knowing that God will give you what God knows
you need in God's good time.

To be turned into fire,
you must pray only for daily bread,
for yourself
and for lavish riches for others.
Enough for yourself
and great blessings for them.

To be turned into fire,
you must spend time with God,
getting to know and love what God fashioned in
your mother's womb.

To be turned into fire,
you must give without counting the cost
"good measure, pressed down and running over."

To be turned into fire,
you must act on what you pray,
your life must be consistent with the word of
God.
You cannot, in other words,
pray for your enemies and support war;
pray to be forgiven and harbor resentment;
pray so that God's reign many come on earth
and not do all in your power to eradicate poverty,
to stand against injustice, to protect human
rights.

How do you know if you're becoming fire?
How do you know if you're melting into pure
gold?

Blessed are the pure ones,
Jesus said,
for they shall see God.
And Saint Mechtild of Magdenburg said,
"The day of my spiritual awakening
was the day I saw all things in God
and God in all things."

Being turned into fire,
being melted into pure gold, then,
has something to do with seeing God
in every man and woman, in all created things
and being transformed into a person
so transparent that others see the flame of God
shining through you.

Picture the three young men
from the Book of Daniel,
dancing and praising God, unharmed,
in the midst of a blazing furnace.
What the onlookers see
when they look in is
"a young man with the face of God."

The hope of this prayerbook,
The Fire of Peace,
is that it may help each of you
dance in the flames of love
until you become burning love itself.

— *Mary Lou Kownacki, OSB*

Prayers for
Life's Journey

FOR PEACE AND GUIDANCE

For Inner Peace

May God support us all the day long,
till the shadows lengthen
and the evening comes
and the busy world is hushed
and the fever of life is over
and our work is done —
then in God's mercy —
may God give us a safe lodging
and a holy rest
and peace at the last.

— attributed to John Henry Newman

Let nothing disturb thee
Let nothing frighten thee
Everything is changing
God alone is changeless
Patience attains the goal
One who has God lacks nothing
God alone fills all our needs.

— Saint Teresa of Avila

For Discontent

Come God!
Do not smile and say
you are already with us.
Millions do not know you
and to us who do,
what is the difference?
What is the point
of your presence
if our lives do not alter?
Change our lives, shatter
our complacency.
Make your word
flesh of our flesh,
blood of our blood
and our life's purpose.
Take away the quietness
of a clear conscience.
Press us uncomfortably.
For only thus
that other peace is made,
your peace.

— Dom Helder Camara

For Inner Tranquility

O God, why must I struggle every day and every hour to secure that inner peace and deep tranquility which is the very essence of what You desire for me and all Your children?

Is it my pride or my passions which make true peace an infrequent visitor in my life? Or, is it your will to seek the purification of my soul by keeping me in disquiet?

The saints have thundered for centuries — let nothing affright you. But oh God, many things do disturb and frighten me. I beg You for deliverance from the demons. I beseech You to give me that peace which You promised to those who at least tried to love You.

St. Ignatius and all the mystics have insisted that unhappiness is not a message from God, but a sign from the Evil One. So, I ask you, God, to dispel the sources of Satan and deliver this pilgrim from turmoil and trouble.

In quietness, tranquility and peace let me just rest in Your peaceful presence until the storms of life subside and the vision of Your beauty is all there is. Amen.

— *Robert F. Drinan, SJ*

6

For Calm

Now,
O God,
calm me into a quietness
    that heals
        and listens,
and molds my longings
    and passions,
        my wounds
                and wonderings
into a more holy
    and human
        shape.

— *Guerrillas of Grace*

O Lord, open my eyes that I may see the
needs of others, open my ears that I may hear
their cries, open my heart so that they need not
be without comfort. Let me not be afraid to
defend the weak because of the anger of the rich.
Show me where love and hope and faith are
needed, and use me to bring them to these
places. Open my eyes and ears that I may, this
coming day, be able to do some work of peace for
Thee.

— *Alan Paton*

I am Peace
surrounded by Peace
secure in Peace.
Peace protects me
Peace supports me
Peace is in me
Peace is mine — All is well.
Peace to all beings
Peace among all beings
Peace from all beings
I am steeped in Peace
Absorbed in Peace
In the streets, at our work,
having peaceful thoughts,
Peaceful words, peaceful acts.

— *A Buddhist meditation*

Lord, make me an instrument of your peace;
Where there is hatred, let me sow love;
Where there is injury, pardon;
Where there is doubt, faith;
Where there is despair, hope;
Where there is darkness, light;
Where there is sadness, joy.

O Divine Master,
grant that I may not so much seek
to be consoled, as to console;
to be understood, as to understand;
to be loved, as to love;
for it is in giving that we receive,
it is in pardoning that we are pardoned,
it is in dying (to self) that we are born
to eternal life.

— *Prayer of Saint Francis*

Lead me from death to life,
from falsehood to truth.
Lead me from despair to hope,
from fear to trust.
Lead me from hate to love,
from war to peace.
Let peace fill my heart, my world, my universe.
Amen.

— *Universal Peace Prayer*

A Hebrew Peace Prayer

Eternal wellspring of peace —
May we be drenched with the longing for peace
that we may give ourselves over to peace
until the earth overflows with peace
as living waters overflow the seas.

— *Marcia Falk*

For Nonviolence

God, thank you for your great love
and all that you give to me.
Give me the grace and the courage
to live a life of nonviolence
so that I may be faithful to Jesus.
Send me your Spirit that I may love everyone
as my sister and my brother and not fear anyone.
Help me to be an instrument of your peace;
to respond with love
and not to retaliate with violence;
to accept suffering rather than inflict it;
to live more simply;
to resist death and to choose life
for all your children.
Guide me along the way of nonviolence.

Disarm my heart
and I shall be your instrument
to disarm other hearts.
Lead me, God of nonviolence,
into your reign of love and peace,
where there is no fear and no violence.
In the name of Jesus. Amen.

— *John Dear, SJ*

Peacemaking Prayer

O God, we believe that peacemaking
means planting seeds
even though we may never see the flower,
and that it means never losing sight of the vision
promised by you.
We hold fast to Your Word that
one day swords will be beat into plowshares.
May we, as peacemakers, stake our lives on that
promise.
We ask this through your life-giving Spirit.
Amen.

— *Pax Christi USA*

For Greatness of Heart

Keep us, O God, from all pettiness,
Let us be large in thought, in word, in deed.
Let us be done with fault-finding
    and leave off all self-seeking.
May we put away all pretense
    and meet each other face to face,
        without self-pity and without prejudice.
May we never be hasty in judgment,
    and always generous.
Let us always take time for all things,
and make us grow calm, serene and gentle.
Teach us to put into action our better impulses,
to be straightforward and unafraid.
Grant that we may realize
    that it is the little things of life that create
        differences,
    that in the big things of life
        we are as one.
And, O God, let us not forget to be kind.

    — Queen Mary Stuart

For Abandonment

O God, I freely yield all my freedom to you.
Take my memory, my intellect and my entire
will.
You have given me everything I am or have;
I give it all back to you to stand under your will
alone.
Your love and your grace are enough for me;
I shall ask for nothing more.

— *St. Ignatius Loyola*

God,
I abandon myself into your hands;
to do with me what you will.
Whatever you may do, I thank you:
I am ready for all, I accept all.
Let only your will be done in me,
and in all your creatures —
I wish no more than this, O God.

Into your hands I commend my soul;
I offer it to you with all the love of my heart,
for I love you, God, and so need to give myself,
to surrender myself into your hands
    without reserve
and with boundless confidence
for you are my God.

    — Charles de Foucauld

For Perseverance

Lord Jesus, teach me to be generous;
teach me to serve you as you deserve,
to give and not to count the cost,
to fight and not to heed the wounds,
to toil and not to seek for rest,
to labor and not to seek reward,
except that of knowing that I do your will.

    — St. Ignatius Loyola

For Hope

Surprise us, O God,
for we often expect so little.
Come to us in ways we cannot predict
and come to us in familiar people, experiences
and words.
Keep us from living as if life is repetitious —
but instead fire us with expectation,
knowing that You move toward us;
with life far in excess,
far more abundant than we dare to hope or
dream.
In Christ's name for the sake of the world. Amen.

— *Doris Donnelly*

For Discernment

My Lord God,
I have no idea where I am going,
I do not see the road ahead of me,
I cannot know for certain where it will end.
Nor do I really know myself,
and the fact that I think
I am following your will
does not mean that I am actually doing so.
But I believe
that the desire to please you
does in fact please you.

And I hope I have that desire
in all that I am doing.
I hope that I will never do anything
apart from that desire.
And I know that if I do this
you will lead me by the right road,
though I may know nothing about it.
Therefore I will trust you always
though I may seem to be lost
and in the shadow of death.
I will not fear,
for you are ever with me,
and you will never leave me
to face my perils alone.

— *Thomas Merton*

For Trust in God

God, my mind is not noisy with desires,
    and my heart has satisfied its longing.
I do not care about religion
    or anything that is not you.
I have soothed and quieted my soul,
    like a child at its mother's breast.
My soul is as peaceful as a child
    sleeping in its mother's arms.

— *Psalm 131*
(trans. by Stephen Mitchell)

For Hospitality of the Heart

Welcoming God,
    teach us to be generous
    in offering hospitality.
Help us to be welcoming
    as you are welcoming,
    with reverence and care,
    mindfulness and respect.
May our greetings be marked by sincerity
    and our actions be marked by tenderness.
May all that we do for ourselves and others
    invite happiness and promise delight,
    seek peace and offer healing,
    encourage simplicity and share affection,
    acknowledge faith and extend friendship.
Enlarge our hearts
    to embrace all people with love
    and bless our efforts to be hospitable.

— *Charlotte Zalot, OSB*

FAMILY PRAYERS

For Families

O God,
bind together in your all-embracing love
    every family on earth.
Banish anger and bitterness within them;
nourish forgiveness and peace.
Bestow upon parents such wisdom and
    patience
that they may gently exercise the disciplines of
    love,
and call forth from their children their
    greatest virtue and their highest skill.
Instill in children such independence and
    self-respect
that they may freely obey their parents,
and grow in the joys of companionship.
Open ears to hear the truth within the words
    another speaks;
open eyes to see the reality beneath another's
    appearance;
and make the mutual affection of families a
    sign of your reign,
through Jesus Christ our Lord.

— an Anglican Prayer Book

For Resolving Conflict in the Home

God of Peace,
    how frightening the sounds and actions of
    anger —
    shouting, screaming, hitting, fighting.
Protect those who are victims —
    husbands, wives, children, pets.
Shelter them from harm.
Give hope to the despairing.
Give calm to the unruly.
Replace hatred with love,
    injury with pardon.
Resolve conflict
    and fill the home with peace.

— Charlotte Zalot, OSB

For a Wedding

Jesus, bless this couple
as they publicly offer their vows of mutual love.
In a world torn by discord, they are a sign of
harmony and hope.
In a world of competition, they represent coop-
eration.
In a world of self-interest, they embody self-
sacrifice.

In a world of violence and war, they call us to
the possibility of peace.
They proclaim their covenant even knowing
many others
who were unable to sustain such commitments.
For their courage they look to their faith
in you and in each other.
Do not allow time or circumstances
to erode their courage or dilute their love.
Let them find in their shared love
happiness, growth, and peace.
Make them generous with each other
and with all who need their assistance.
May they continue to be for all of us
a sign of your presence and love.
And may your abundant peace fill their lives
and overflow into our troubled world. Amen.

— *Jim Dinn*

For Pregnant Women

Nurturing God,
    bless all women who have been given
    the gift of life to carry to birth in their
    wombs.
Strengthen them in their bodies.
Still them in their fears.
Sustain them in their waiting.

Put your spirit of peace into their breathing
    and into the children soon to be born.
May their time draw near in joyful hope.
May the mystery and miracle of new life
    fill them with awe.
May your blessing rest upon them.

— *Charlotte Zalot, OSB*

At the Birth of a Child

Jesus, we gratefully celebrate the birth of this
child.
As we stand in awe before the precious mystery
of human life,
help us to treasure this gift
not only in this child but in ourselves
and in our brothers and sisters everywhere.
Empower us to transform our society and our
world
so as to be worthy of this new life.
Bless this child with the love of family and
friends.
May she/he walk in the paths of peace
and live to celebrate and share your peace
with the whole human family. Amen.

— *Jim Dinn*

For a Single Parent

Ever-faithful God,
    bless those who embrace
    the challenge of being both mother and
    father.
Enable them to be firm but gentle,
    strong yet tender.
Let what is achievable be within their reach.
Let what seems insurmountable
    be possible with your help.
Renew their energy.
Revive their enthusiasm.
Remind them that they are not alone.
You, God, are with them.
Be their help.
Be their consolation.
Be their peace.

— *Charlotte Zalot, OSB*

For Children of Separation/Divorce

Compassionate God,
    reach out to those children
    who suffer as a result of separation
    or divorce.
Comfort them in their confusion;
    embrace them in their fear.

Let not their hearts be hardened by loss;
    soften their anger.
Warm them with your love.
Hold them in their vulnerability.
Convince them that someone does care.
You, O God, will not abandon them.
Keep them safe and secure.

— *Charlotte Zalot, OSB*

For an Anniversary

Jesus, our assurance of your presence and
guidance in our lives
is reinforced by our memory of past blessings.
On this anniversary we look back with joy and
gratitude
on another year completed.
In a life of change in a changing world
we are encouraged by the continuing vitality of
our commitment,
and we ask all the more confidently for your
ongoing love and support.
Help us to nurture and sustain all that is good in
one another.
In this coming year let our love be graced
by understanding, fidelity, and peace
so that our next anniversary may celebrate
new depth and fresh delight in our commitment.

May your gift of peace permeate our lives
and enrich everyone that our lives touch. Amen.

— *Jim Dinn*

PRAYERS OF CONCERN

For Those Serving Others

Jesus, our model of service and bringer of peace,
look with love on those who dedicate themselves
to the service of others.
Let these persons, on whom so many depend,
be especially nourished by your supporting
Spirit.
Give them wholeness and holiness in their lives
and bless them with the awareness of the good
they accomplish.
Remove all taint of arrogance or self-pity.
Give them joy in their work
so they may feel privileged and compensated to
share in your role.
Give them an abundance of patience and energy
and gentleness
so that all to whom they minister
may be empowered and dignified by their service.
Let servers and served bestow on each other
a deeper taste of your Spirit's peace. Amen.

— *Jim Dinn*

For the Hungry

Lord Jesus, when you saw the hungry multitudes
you said to your disciples "You feed them yourselves."
Today, dear Jesus, the hungry multitudes
include
an ever growing number of women and children
in our world.
They are as near as our neighbors
and as far away as Africa and Asia.

Just as you instructed the disciples
to take account of what they possessed and begin
sharing with the hungry,
give me the wisdom to number my blessings
and the faith to share my loaves and fishes
with those who have none.

Give me the courage to speak to those in power
on behalf of the hungry, whether they be friend
or foe,
whether they be politically important or inconse-
quential.
As long as there is hunger in the world
may I never grow weary of loving tenderly and
seeking justice.
Amen.

— Tom Cordaro

For the Homeless

Brother Jesus, there was no room in the inn
when you came into the world.
And today there are very few inns of hospitality
for the homeless in our cities, our nation and our
world.
Create room in my heart for the homeless
whose lives are uprooted
and whose days are spent searching for a resting
place.
Give me welcoming hands and listening ears
that I might create in my life
a place of comfort and refuge for them.
Give me a courageous voice and the strength
needed
to work with the homeless as they struggle
for dignity and a dwelling place in our communities.
And give me the eyes to recognize you in the
faces
of the refugees of war, political persecution
and economic hard times. Amen.

— *Tom Cordaro*

For Political Prisoners

Almighty God,
you sent Jesus
to bring to the whole world
the glorious liberty
of the children of God.
Open the eyes
of those responsible
for unjust imprisonment, for torture
and for abuse of human rights
to the blindness of their actions.
Open the way of perseverance and freedom
to those in prison
for reason of conscience.
Open the hearts of your faithful
to receive the liberating power of your Spirit.
Amen.

For Refugees

Jesus,
you were forced to flee into Egypt
to avoid political persecution
and know well the pain and suffering of refugees.
Remember in your mercy
refugees who have lost home and land,
who are threatened by disease and hunger,
who are separated from their families.

Jesus, the refugee,
we ask you to direct the minds of politicians
and the hearts of all people
so that the sufferings
of the displaced are relieved
and their sorrows healed.

For Those Who Minister to the Poor

You will find that charity
is a heavy burden
to carry, heavier than
the kettle of soup
and the basket of bread.

But you must your gentleness
and your smile keep.

Giving soup and bread isn't all
that the rich can do.

The poor are your masters
terribly sensitive: exacting
as you will see.

But the uglier and dirtier they are
the more unjust and bitter
the more you must give them your love.

It is only because of your love —
    only your love —
that the poor will forgive you
the bread you give them.

    — *St. Vincent de Paul*

For Health Care for the Needy

Christ Jesus,
you did not turn away
from the Canaanite woman
who begged you to heal her daughter.
Open our hearts
to hear the cry of those who are sick
and have no money for treatment.
Help us to change our country's priorities
so that more funds are available
for works of healing than for weapons of war.
Teach us to respect our bodies
and care for them as temples of your Holy Spirit.
Help us to see
that we are all members of the same body
and that when one member is ill, we all suffer.
Amen.

    — *Tom Cordaro*

For Those Enslaved to Drugs

Brother Jesus, you said,
"God has anointed me;
God has sent me to bring
good news to the poor,
to heal the brokenhearted,
to proclaim liberty to captives
and release to prisoners,
to announce a year of favor from God
and a day of vindication by our God,
to comfort all who mourn."
Come, heal our brothers and sisters
who are trapped
in the deadly grasp of drug addiction.
Set free our communities
held hostage to fear and mistrust.
Give us the grace and courage
to announce a year of favor from God
and a day of vindication,
as we rebuild our communities,
rebuild our schools,
and rebuild the lives and dreams
of our young people. Amen.

— *Tom Cordaro*

For the Church

Dear God,
we are all too conscious
of in-fighting, bickering, power plays, jealousies
that keep the church from being about Your
business.
More often than not,
even when grateful for a faithful, functioning
church,
we call it peaceful or harmonious
and miss the dynamism, the life-force,
the productive tension that keeps the church
alive, quickened and perhaps open to Your
transforming spirit.
May we continue to confront and affirm one
another,
to live for each other in Christ's name.
Keep us mindful, O God,
that we need to be concerned
with human structures and ideas,
plans and programs,
visions and dreams — but do You,
most gracious God, center us on the source of
life,

the essence of the church,
the place we have in the plan which You have
shown us in Jesus Christ,
called us to live in,
and empowered us to share. Amen.

— *Doris Donnelly*

For the Criminal

Jesus, you were counted among thieves
and you were the victim of capital punishment.
Yet you came to set free those who are imprisoned.
Heal the souls of those who, in their pain,
inflict suffering on others.
Help us to see ourselves in the face of the criminal.
Forgive us our sins,
as we forgive the sins of those who have tres-
passed against us.
Give us the power not to punish but to heal,
not to seek retribution but to work for restora-
tion
and the reign of your shalom. Amen.

— *Tom Cordaro*

For Racial Harmony

Creator God,
you have made of one blood
all races and nations.
Increase among us the spirit of sympathy and
understanding,
of tolerance and goodwill;
that the prejudice, arrogance and pride
which causes division between those
of different race or color
may be done away with,
and all peoples may live together in unity and
peace. Amen.

For the Victims of Crime

Rescuer God, Healing Spirit,
hear the cry of those who fall victim
to the violence of crime.
Move us, as you did the Good Samaritan,
to pour ointment on their pain,
to bind their wounds, to cover their shame
and to hold them in our hearts
until they are whole again.
Come to the aid of our communities,
so filled with fear and violence.

Help us to overcome our fears
with a loving concern for one another
as we build your reign of peace. Amen.

— *Tom Cordaro*

Saint Martin of Tours Prayer for COs

Blessed Martin of Tours,
as a soldier in the Roman army
you opened your heart
to the nonviolent message
of Jesus and refused to bear arms.

Comfort and strengthen young people
of the United States Armed Forces
who for reasons of conscience
cannot participate in war.
May we imitate your example
and always follow the law written
on our hearts. Give us courage to obey
the dictates of conscience in all circumstances,
even when the voice within
conflicts with the law of the land.

Enable all who refuse to bear arms
feel our love and support.
Inspire our government leaders

to grant amnesty to all conscientious objectors.
Amen.

— *Pax Christi USA*

For the United Nations

O God
it is your will
that all men and women
live together as brothers and sisters.
Give wisdom and understanding
to all who work through the United Nations.
Grant them a sense of unity and purpose
as they strive
to build a world of righteousness and peace.

For Government Officials

God, we do believe that government leaders
can talk their way through conflicts, but how
hard it is to hold on to that belief. Free us from
cynicism.

Jesus, Word of God, teach world leaders how
to listen, how to speak out of experiences that
bond and unite them.

When leaders negotiate, may they know that
we are with them, bringing our gifts of prayer
and fasting, gratitude and hope.

We dream of the day when war is no more, when conversation and negotiation have replaced military threats and missile targets. May our dream become flesh and dwell among us. Amen.

— *Mary Evelyn Jegen, SND*

For the United States

How grateful we are, O God,
  for our great country,
  for the blessings you lavish upon our land.
How concerned we are, O God,
  that our very nation may become our god
  and that we worship the gifts
  rather than the Giver.
Is it possible, O God,
  that our law may circumvent your will
  that our freedom may place chains on others
  that our wealth may impoverish some
  that our power may come by way of
  another's weakness
  that our enemies may be those
  who are obedient to you?
Dare we pray, O God,
  that you take away those things that
  come between us and you?

— *Leslie Brandt*

For the Unemployed

Jesus, your compassion could not let a crowd go home hungry.
Look with that same compassion on the unemployed.
Some of them are hungry;
some need clothes;
some need shelter.
Many have families who depend upon them.
Help them all to meet these needs now
while they are unemployed,
and help then soon to find suitable work.
Above all, in a world that too easily measures a person's worth
by income and job title,
confirm them, Jesus, in the awareness
of their own dignity and worth.
Do not let the lack of a job diminish them
in their eyes or anyone else's.
Give them loyal and supportive friends.
Safeguard them against bitterness and discouragement.
Let even this painful experience deepen their faith
and align their priorities more closely with yours.

Finally, guide us all to build the social structures
that will enable more persons to earn their living
in ways that promote human dignity
and contribute to the common good. Amen.

— Jim Dinn

For our Country

Living God,
we praise you
for the abundance of this land,
for the gifts of its peoples,
for the potential of its resources.
You have given us
everything we need
to make life good
and beautiful for all.

We confess to being unfaithful stewards.
We repent for the sin of colonialism
which denied so many
the right to use the same resources,
to enjoy the same fruits of their labors.

Forgive us our arrogance, intolerance
and even cruelty
toward those whose traditions, beliefs
and cultures differ from our own.

Send us the redeeming, healing and
liberating power
needed to work as sisters and brothers
with all peoples of the world
for human community as you meant it to be.
Amen.

— *Pax Christi USA*

For the Human Family

Creator God,
you have made all of us.
Red, yellow, brown, white and black,
tall and short, fat and thin,
rich and poor, young and old —
are all your children.
Teach us to cooperate rather than to compete,
to respect rather than to revile,
to forgive rather than to condemn.
Your Son turned from no one.
May we learn, like him, to be open
to the share of the divine
that you have implanted
in each of your sons and daughters.

And may we forge a bond of love
that will make a living reality
the sisterhood and brotherhood in which
    we profess to believe.

   — *The Christophers*

For the Earth

Creator God,
help us to harness
the wind
the water
the sun
and all the ready
and renewable
sources of power.

Teach us to conserve
preserve
use wisely
the blessed treasures
of our wealth-stored earth.

Help us to share
your bounty
not to waste it
or pervert it
into peril
for our children
or our neighbors
in other nations.

You who are life
and energy
and blessing,
teach us to reverence
and respect
your tender world.

— *Thomas John Carlisle*

PRAYERS OF PRAISE

In Praise of God

Holy is God!
Holy and strong One.
holy immortal One.
have mercy on us.

For the Work of our Hands

Blessed be the works of your hands,
    O Holy One.
Blessed be these hands that have touched life.
Blessed be these hands that have nurtured
creativity.
Blessed be these hands that have held pain.
Blessed be these hands that have embraced with
passion.
Blessed be these hands that have tended gar-
dens.
Blessed be these hands that have closed in
anger.
Blessed be these hands that have planted new
seeds.
Blessed be these hands that have harvested ripe
fields.

Blessed be these hands that have cleaned,
washed, mopped and scrubbed.
Blessed be these hands that have become
gnarled with age.
Blessed be these hands that are wrinkled and
scarred from doing justice.
Blessed be these hands that have reached out
and been received.
Blessed be these hands that hold the promise of
the future.
Blessed be the works of your hands,
    O Holy One.

    — Diann Neu

For Beauty

God of Creation,
    open our eyes, our ears,
    our minds, our hearts,
    our bodies, our bones,
    to the beauty that is within and without.
Help us not be blind
    to the goodness that surrounds us
    or deaf to the sounds that resonate inside us.
You reveal yourself daily
    through the radiant splendor of your creation
    and the design of your heart.

May we be mindful of our responsibility
    to not only appreciate magnificence
    but to co-create it as well.
May a more beautiful world
    be the challenge of our peace-making
    and the desire of our hearts.

    — *Charlotte Zalot, OSB*

For Life's Journey

Now Talking God
With your feet I walk
I carry forth your body
For me your mind thinks
Your voice speaks for me
Beauty is before me
And beauty is behind me
Above and below me hovers the beautiful
I am surrounded by it
I am immersed in it
In my youth I am aware of it
And in old age I shall walk quietly
The beautiful trail.

    — *Native American Prayer*

For Goodness

Blessed are the man and the woman
    who have grown beyond their greed
    and have put an end to their hatred
    and no longer nourish illusions.
But they delight in the way things are
    and keep their hearts open, day and night.
They are like trees planted near flowing rivers,
    which bear fruit when they are ready.
Their leaves will not fall or wither.
    Everything they do will succeed.

— Psalm 1
(trans. by Stephen Mitchell)

For Humanity

Our Father, Mother, who are in the world and
    surpass the world,
Blessed be your presence, in us, in animals
    and flowers, in still air and wind.
May justice and peace dwell among us, as you
    come to us.
Your will be our will;
You will that we be sisters and brothers, as
    bread is bread, water is itself,
For our hunger, for quenching of thirst.
Forgive us.

We walk crookedly in the world, are perverse,
    and fail of our promise.
But we would be human, if only you consent to
    stir up our hearts.
Amen.

    — Daniel Berrigan, SJ

For the Ordinary

When we consider your world, O God,
we always seem to be aware of the bizarre,
the out-of-kilter, the extraordinary.
Only occasionally do we marvel
at day following night,
at the repeating cycles of birth, growth,
    decay and death,
at the consistency of the phases of the moon.
Give us the grace to wonder at the ordinary.

    — Doris Donnelly

Shantytown Woman's Canticle

My being proclaims much suffering, O God,
my spirit is oppressed and trampled upon.
I have been a slave for generations,
and all ages have considered me less than man.

Wonderful God, you have created me,
Holy are you, Holy am I.
Your goodness is never-ending to those who seek
you.

Our Father and our Mother
we have boxed you up.
The mighty will someday meet you
and cry bitter tears
from their courts.

By my poverty,
I know I'm forgiven
and can rest
in your arms.

Bread many times
is not on our table,
while the rich
eat cake in darkness.

You hold the world's women dear,
because the promise and hope for a new day
reside in a compassionate heart,
since the time Mary visited Elizabeth,
since Bethlehem
and since standing at Calvary.

And women visited women and returned home
new.

— Carolyn Lehmann, M.M.

Canticle of Brother Sun and Sister Moon

Most high, almighty, good God!
  All praise, glory, honor and exaltation
      are yours!
  To you alone do they belong,
  and no mere mortal dares pronounce
      your Name.

Praise to you, O God, for all
          your creatures:
  first, for our dear Brother Sun,
  who gives us the day
  and illumines us with his light;
  fair is he, in splendor radiant,
  bearing your very likeness, O God.

For our Sister Moon,
  and for the bright, shining stars:
  We praise you, O God.

For our Brother Wind,
  for fair and stormy seasons
  and all heaven's varied moods,
  by which you nourish all that you have
      made:
  We praise you, O God.

For our Sister Water,
   so useful, lowly, precious and pure:
   We praise you, O God.

For our Brother Fire,
   who brightens up our darkest nights:
   beautiful is he and eager,
   invincible and keen:
   We praise you, O God.

For our Mother Earth,
   who sustains and feeds us,
   producing fair fruits, many-colored
         flowers and herbs:
   We praise you, O God.

For those who forgive one another for
love of you,
and who patiently bear sickness and
         other trials.
Happy are they who peacefully
         endure;
   you will crown them, O Most High:
   We praise you, O God.

For our Sister Death,
   the inescapable fact of life
   Woe to those who die in mortal sin!
   Happy those she finds doing your
         will!

From the Second Death they stand
       immune:
We praise you, O God.

All creatures,
    praise and glorify my God
    and give God thanks
    and serve God in great humility.

WE PRAISE YOU, O GOD.

          — St. Francis of Assisi
          (trans. W.G.S.)

For the Earth's Blessings

O God, Creator of heaven and earth

May it please You to grant favorable weather,
temperate rain, and fruitful seasons, that there
may
be food and drink for all your children.

May it please You to bless the fields, farms,
forests and the water springs of all lands,
and to bless all who work there to bring forth
food
needed by your people.

May it please You to draw all peoples
to enjoy and value the natural world
in which you have placed us.

May it please You to look with favor
on all who care for the earth, its waters and its
skies,
that the riches of Your creation may be enjoyed
from generation to generation. Amen

— *Synapses*

SPECIAL PEOPLE, SPECIAL EVENTS

For Students

All-knowing God,
    illuminate the minds
    and hearts of those who study.
May all that they learn
    help them to act justly,
    love tenderly,
    and walk humbly
    with you, their God.
Give them the discipline
    to learn well.
Give them the desire
    to be open.
Give them the depth
    to absorb your teaching.
Stretch their understanding.
Delight their intellect.
Bless their determination
    with firm purpose
    and guide them
    in your ways of peace.

— *Charlotte Zalot, OSB*

For Teachers

God of Enlightenment,
    bless those who teach.
By their commitment
    they lead many
    from darkness to light.
By their dedication
    they lead many
    from fear to trust.
By their perseverance
    they lead many
    from falsehood to truth.
Gift them with continued insight
    and confidence
    to guide those whom they teach
    in the ways of peace and justice.
Let them inspire others
    by their faithfulness.
Let them challenge others
    by their purpose.
Let them enliven others
    by their enthusiasm.
Blessed are teachers who nurture life.

— Charlotte Zalot, OSB

For Artists, Musicians, Poets, Film Makers

God of All Goodness,
    your creative energy flows
    through artists, musicians, poets, and film
    makers.
Their gifts of art, music, poetry and films
    broaden our vision to encompass beauty
    that may have otherwise been missed.
Splendor is comprehended through their works
    as delight is experienced in the joy of music
    or the pleasure of poetry.
May the ongoing sharing of their gifts
    be encouraged by
    appreciative eyes and grateful ears
    in a world that is in need
    of loveliness and life.

— *Charlotte Zalot, OSB*

For Youth

God of Energy,
    enliven the youth of our day
    with the promise of faithful companionship.
Call them to partnership with you
    in the creation of a new world.
Keep their hearts filled
    with excitement and adventure.

Help them be open to change
    and all that is new.
Challenge them creatively
    and give success to the work of their hands.
They are our trust.
They are our hope.
They are our future.
Give them a profound reverence
    for all that is right and good.
Be their guard and guide.

— *Charlotte Zalot, OSB*

For People in the Media

Dear God, you inspired the first evangelists
to write the Good News
so all people might come to know the truth
and the truth might set them free.

Today, the news that comes to us is seldom good
and it is difficult to discern
whether those who control the news
are committed to revealing truth
or more interested in making profits.
Give me the wisdom to distinguish
entertainment from information,
and advertisement from analysis.

Give those who decide what is news
the grace and courage to bring light
to the great issues we face as a nation
and as citizens of the world.

I pray especially for those journalists
who work for small underfunded newspapers,
    journals and radio stations.
They are often the ones that bring to light
the stories that the powerful want to keep in the
dark.
Grant them, O God, the grace to continue their
difficult work
and make me aware of the importance of supporting them.

— Tom Cordaro

For the Rich

Jesus, your heart went out to the rich young
man.
You loved his earnestness and understood his
struggles.
You also recognized and were saddened
by the paralyzing power that possessions held
over him.
Liberate any rich persons who are in bondage to
their wealth.

Help them achieve the liberty of spirit that is
beyond price
so that they may be unrestrained in their
generosity.
Let them experience their solidarity with the
poor and suffering
so that they may experience more deeply
your love and your peace.
Touch our own hearts
so we will not be blinded by the wealth of others
into undervaluing their generosity
or judging them too severely.
To the extent that any of us are rich, or seem
rich to others,
look on us as you looked on that rich young man,
and free us from the bondage of possessions.
Give us open and responsive hearts
that we may generously share what we have
gratefully received.
Help us and all humankind to recognize and
celebrate
our oneness as your children united in your
Spirit of peace. Amen.

— *Jim Dinn*

For the Lonely

Jesus, you called all people to fellowship
with you and one another.
You invite us all to experience and express
the inclusive love that was your special gift.
Embrace the lonely.
Whether they live in solitude or in solidarity,
touch their hearts with love.
If they feel isolated, bond them with affection.
If they feel rejected, let them be reconciled.
If they feel deprived, let them know wholeness.
If they mourn, give them comfort.
If they need understanding, let them experience
the respect and acceptance that they crave.
Transform them with your love
so they may know your peace
and discover they are not alone.
Draw them and all of us into closer communion
with you and with each other, in peace. Amen.

— Jim Dinn

For Someone Dying

Jesus, be with those we love as they approach
death.
Let the faith and prayers of all believers support
them.
Free them from fear. Ease their pain.

Do not let them be burdened by the thought
of separation from family and friends.
Let them find courage and comfort in the knowledge
that even in this experience of death
they are not separated from you.
Deepen their faith. Drive out anxiety
about the people and concerns they will leave
behind
and fill them with the awareness of your love.
Reconcile them in spirit with anyone they have
offended
and anyone who has offended them.
And may their entrance into death
bring them to a fuller sharing in your peace.
Amen.

— Jim Dinn

For the Beginning of a Peace Meeting

Dear God, our boat is so small
and the sea is so wide and deep.
We are only a small group of people
and the challenges we face
are vast and overwhelming.

Sometimes we begin to panic
as the waves of injustice and violence
break over the bow of our ship
While you seem to sleep in our midst.
Sometimes it seems that we are not moving at
all when the winds of your Spirit grow silent.

Dear God, be with us this day
as we chart our course towards peace and justice.
May your Holy Spirit bring fair winds and a
clear sky to our discernment and plans of action.
Calm our fears and anxiousness
as you calm the waters around us.
Grant us your peace and make us
one of heart, mind and spirit. Amen.

— *Tom Cordaro*

For the End of a Peace Meeting

Thank you dear God for bringing us together this
day.
Thank you for the gifts we as individuals
bring to our community of concern and
the power we have when we join together
to seek your way of peace with justice.

Please accept our meager offerings
of time, talent and treasure
as our prayer for a more just and peaceful world.
Take what little we offer and make it grow
until it brings forth the fruit of justice and peace
in our lives, in our community and in our world.
Amen.

—*Tom Cordaro*

After a Discussion

We dare to believe, O God,
that there has been purpose in our being together.
For each comment and question offered,
for the risks taken,
for the efforts made to search for truth,
and for the grace extended
when another viewpoint wounded or angered —
for every insight that called us to reconsider
our motives and intentions,
we give you thanks.
Forgive us we pray
for any unwillingness or lack of discipline
that undercut what we might have been
or done together in your name.

May your Spirit
sustain us in our grateful acceptance of Your
mercy,
empower us to forgive ourselves and each other,
and provoke a renewed commitment to live as
Christ's body
in your world. Amen.

— *Doris Donnelly*

Before Reading Scripture

O God, whose Word comes to me in so many
ways, be with me today
as I ponder your Word in Scripture.
Speak to me that I may hear Your words afresh.
Open my heart that it might be filled with Your
words of love.
Strengthen me as I seek to live out Your Word
in acts of love and kindness and justice toward
my neighbor. Amen.

— *National Council of Churches*

For Meals

Creator of the Universe, the seas, the stars —
We gather this day for our daily bread.
Out of the earth
you bring forth rain so grain will grow,
you bring forth sun so fruit will grow.

We bless and promise to protect
all that nourishes growth
    in the earth
    in our spirits and
    in our world.

As we share this food
we remember our interdependence with each
other and with the earth.
Let there be only good times between us.
In the name of your Spirit. Amen.

— *Author unknown*

For Retirement

Peaceful God, you left your work of creation
incomplete
so that countless generations of women and men
could share in its continuation.

Give me the gift of peace
to accept and enjoy retirement
without being anxious
about family needs
or my health or my former job.
Let me treasure my happy memories of work:
the shared experiences and personal achieve-
ments.
Let time soften the memories of whatever was
painful or unpleasant.
Give me enthusiasm and purpose for today and
tomorrow.
Teach me new ways to grow and to help others
grow.
Let me learn now, if I have not learned already,
how to relax, how to enjoy life, and how to pray.
With these gifts I can be content
with myself, with friends, and with you.
Be close to me in these years
so that I may more deeply taste your peace
and more effectively communicate it to others.
Amen.

— *Jim Dinn*

For Graduation

Spirit of Wisdom, whose truth fills our world
and invites us into a lifetime of learning,
bless these graduates.

Give them joy and a sense of accomplishment in
what they have achieved.
But give them also a thirst for knowledge.
Make them seekers who will enjoy the process of
discovery.
Let their education go beyond classrooms and
books.
Sensitize them to the lessons of experience and
the wisdom of the heart.
Open them to faith as well as reason, intuition
as well as logic.
Give them a curiosity that goes beyond partial
answers and old insights.
But through all their life give them an inner
peace
so they are neither inflated by what they know
nor frustrated by what is still beyond their
grasp.
Abiding teacher, may this graduation that we
celebrate today
signal the beginning of their larger education.
Bless them and all of us with your wisdom and
peace. Amen.

— *Jim Dinn*

For a Vacation

Loving creative Spirit, model and source of peace
and restfulness,
bless my vacation.
Do not let me waste this opportunity for relaxation.
Protect me against whatever would spoil it.
Free me from the preoccupations and pressures
and anxieties
that are connected to my daily work.
Heal in me whatever has been wounded or
broken.
Revive whatever has been stifled or buried.
Renew my spirit.
Let this be a time of refreshment,
a time of growing inner peace.
Increase my capacity for enjoyment
and let me be truly re-created
so I may in the future offer less resistance
to your penetrating power. Amen.

— *Jim Dinn*

For a Birthday

Creator God, you are the loving source of all
existence,
the father and mother of all life.

You continually invite me to grow and develop in
your image.
With joy and gratitude I celebrate another year
completed.
As I look back and remember the blessings
already received,
I also look ahead and confidently ask for your
continuing gifts.
Do not permit the passing of time to be a burden;
let it never diminish or dull my openness to life.
Let me experience in fuller measure each year
the love of family and friends,
harmony with all persons,
and the beautiful unity of your creation.
May each passing year bring me to a deeper faith
and a fuller participation in your gifts of the
Spirit and peace. Amen.

— *Jim Dinn*

For Reconciliation after an Argument

Loving Creator, you call us to be reflections of
your love.
You invite us to accept and share
your gifts of forgiveness and peace.
Reach out to us as we feel the pain and shame
of separation because of disagreement.
Do not let our hurt feeling become an excuse
to brood over injuries or build walls.

Keep us always open to the possibility that we
may be wrong,
and help us to learn from others' point of view.
Give us a readiness to forgive and to accept
forgiveness.
After our disagreement bring us together in
mutual healing love
so that, as your reconciled children,
we may enjoy and communicate your gift of
peace. Amen.

— *Jim Dinn*

For a Promotion

Jesus, I praise and thank you
for this promotion that I have received.
You know that I sometimes need praise and
recognition
to encourage and energize me.
You know also the ways I can use the higher
salary.
Help me to adjust to the expanded responsibili-
ties.
Enable me to grow into the role without anxiety
or compromise.

But save me, Jesus, from the trap
of measuring myself by my place on a career
ladder.
Don't let me envy those with authority over me
nor think less of those over whom I have authority.
Don't let me be hostage to the lure of money or
power.
Keep me from sacrificing personal and family
values to ambition.
Help me find in my promotion an empowerment
and expanded scope for service.
Let the recognition of my talents and contribu-
tions
liberate me from self-doubts
and complement your gift of inner peace. Amen.

— *Jim Dinn*

For Work

May my mind think no harm,
may my lips speak no harm,
may my hands do no harm.
May the children of tomorrow
bless the work I offer.

— *Mary Lou Kownacki, OSB*

For Vocations to Peacemaking

Dear God, the harvest is plenty and the laborers
are few.
Your people long for peace, they thirst for justice.
Send into our midst women and men whose
hearts
can embrace the entire world.
Send into our midst young and old
whose arms can lift up the lowly and oppressed.
Send into our midst rich and poor
who will walk with the powerless as they
struggle for justice.
Send into our midst people of all color
who can see a brother or sister in the eyes of a
stranger.
Send us peacemakers, O God, send us your
peace. Amen.

— *Tom Cordaro*

For Going to Trial after Civil Disobedience

Brother Jesus, in warning us of the trials ahead
you said we would be brought before the courts
to give witness on account of the gospel.
You told us not to worry about our defense
and you promised to give us words and wisdom
that our adversaries would not be able to refute.

Send forth your Spirit now
and grant me the wisdom you promised.
Let me not be boastful or condescending
but give me the courage
to speak of your name and your Good News.
Keep my heart from fear of the judicial process
by helping me to see beyond the
legal formalities and symbols of human power
to the One who will judge us all.
Amen.

— *Tom Cordaro*

Imprisonment after Civil Disobedience

Saving Jesus, who suffered the humiliation of
imprisonment,
come to me now in the hour of my need,
for my heart is filled with fear and anguish
as I contemplate my own imprisonment.

What will become of me, O God?
Do not abandon me to the darkness of the pit.
Do not cut me off from the land of the living.

The psalmist says "if I sink to the nether world,
you are present there... for darkness itself is not
dark and night shines as the day."

Be my light in the darkness of my prison cell,
and help me to see your light in the eyes of my
fellow prisoners.

Give me the courage to be vulnerable to all I
meet
so that in my weakness your loving power might
be known.
Give me the virtues of patience and long-suffer-
ing
that I might be light to all who live in darkness.
Never leave my side Dear God. Amen.

— *Tom Cordaro*

Before Participating in a Peace Demonstration

Jesus,
When the Pharisees tried to silence the people
who lined the streets of Jerusalem
shouting "Hosanna" to your name and rule
you said, "If they were to keep silence
I tell you the very stones would cry out!"
I ask you to help me
break the silence which allows injustice and
violence to reign.
Give me the courage to publicly proclaim your
reign
and to witness to your truth.

Create in me a clean heart, that I might demon-
strate
your nonviolent love for all people.
Guard my heart, hands and tongue
so that in everything I do I will give testimony
to the coming of the nonviolent God of peace
with justice.
And open the hearts of those I witness to
as you open my heart to them.
Amen.

— *Tom Cordaro*

Prayer for Consolation

Jesus, you were always moved
by the sorrow of those touched by death.
You knew the pain of separation, the power of
grief.
You felt the heavy weight of loneliness and the
sense of loss.
Heal these friends and relatives who are in
mourning.
Let them feel no shame for their tears.
But give them the love and comfort of friends to
sustain them.
Grant them faith deep enough to accept even
death
with the assurance that it is the prelude
to our sharing in your resurrection and new life.

Give to these who mourn
an early and deep experience
of the comfort you promised to those who grieve.
Let them know the boundlessness of your mercy
and love
toward them and toward the one they mourn.
Draw them gently out of their grief
into a fuller sharing in the life and service
of your community of believers. Amen.

— Jim Dinn

Daily Prayers
for Ordinary Time

Compiled by Marilyn Schauble, OSB
and Charlotte Zalot, OSB.

MONDAY

Morning

Call to Prayer
I reverence God
in the dawning light.

Antiphon
O God, I cry out to you in the morning;
in you is the source of light and life.

Psalm 27
O God, you are my saving light;
in your presence I am not fearful.
You protect my life, freeing me from fear.

When the violent seek to oppress me,
seek to tear me down,
they themselves stumble and fall,
while my heart remains undaunted.

There is one thing I ask of you;
for this I long:
to live in your house
all the days of my life.

You provide me with a safe place,
build a shelter to protect me.
In you I find refuge from the violent.
My heart praises you in song and dance.

Caught up in your beauty,
I speak of my heart's desire:
to find the fullness of life,
dwelling in your presence forever.

Without you I am lonely and desolate;
do not reject me.
You are my heart's consolation;
there is no other.

Teach me to follow
the path that leads to you.
My oppressors plan violence against me;
false witnesses speak my name maliciously.

Your goodness fills my life.
In fidelity of heart I wait,
I wait to share the vision of your love,
to savor the sweetness of your presence.

Reading

Make no mistake about this, my dear friends.
Every worthwhile gift, every genuine benefit
comes from above, descending from the God of
the heavenly luminaries, who cannot change and
who is never shadowed over. God wills to bring
us to birth with a word spoken in truth so that
we may be a kind of first fruits of creation. Keep
this in mind, dear friends.   (James 1:16-19)

Reflection

As God's Word unfolds
it gives light.

Prayer

God, in your tender compassion
the morning sun will rise
giving light to those in darkness
and guiding all in ways of peace.

Evening

Call to Prayer

I reverence God
who knows my need.

Antiphon

In you I trust, O God;
be not far from me.

Psalm 23

You are my shepherd, O God;
there is nothing I shall want.

Fresh and green are the pastures
where you give me repose.
Near restful waters you lead me,
refreshing my spirit.

You guide me along safe paths;
you are true to your name.
Though I walk in the valley of darkness,
no evil do I fear.
Your rod and staff comfort me.

You prepare a banquet for me
in the sight of my enemies.
My head you anoint with oil;
my cup overflows.

Surely, goodness and kindness
shall follow me
all the days of my life.
I shall dwell in your house forever.

Reading

On that day this song will be sung in the land of Judah: "We have a strong city. You, God, set up walls and ramparts to protect us. Open the gates to let in a nation that is just, one that keeps faith. A nation of firm purpose you keep in peace for its trust in you." Trust in God forever, for God is an eternal Rock!   (Isaiah 26:1-4)

Reflection

As God's Word unfolds
it gives comfort.

Prayer

God, give comfort to those who trust
in you and fill all hearts with peace.

Tuesday

Morning

Call to Prayer
> I reverence God
> with words of praise.

Antiphon
> Blessed be God's name forever.

Psalm 34
> I will bless God
> with constant words of praise.
> I glory in God alone;
> let the humble hear and rejoice.
>
> Revere the Holy One;
> together let us sing praise.
> I seek the God of Life who answers me;
> from all my fears I am set free.
>
> Look toward God and be radiant.
> The poor called and were heard;
> they were rescued from all their distress.
>
> The angel of God surrounds the faithful.
> Drink in the richness of God;
> this presence gives comfort and hope.

Live in awe of God, all you holy ones;
and you will lack nothing.

Who longs for a life filled with blessing
and many days to enjoy prosperity?
Come, beloved, and hear me;
learn to cherish God.

Keep your tongue from evil
and your lips from speaking deceit.
Do not yield to evil but embrace goodness.
Seek and strive for lasting peace.

God turns from the wicked
to destroy any remembrance of them.
God turns to the just and hears their appeal;
they shall be saved.

God is close to the broken-hearted;
those whose spirit is crushed will be saved.
The just will be rescued from all their
     trials.
God will watch over them,
so not one of their bones will be broken.

Evil brings death to the wicked;
those who hate the good are doomed.
No one who takes refuge in God
     shall be condemned.

Reading

I plead with you, then, as a prisoner for Christ,
to live a life worthy of the calling you have
received, with perfect humility, meekness, and
patience, bearing with one another lovingly.
Make every effort to preserve the unity which
has the Spirit as its origin and peace as its
binding force.   (Ephesians 4:1-3)

Reflection

As God's Word unfolds
it gives challenge.

Prayer

God, your saving help gives reason for
praise. Through your kindness may all
stand unshaken.

Evening

Call to Prayer

I reverence God
in whose faithfulness I take refuge.

Antiphon

God remembers a merciful love
for those who are of pure heart.

Psalm 16

Preserve me, God, I take shelter in you.
I say to you,/ "You are my god.
My happiness lies in you alone."

You place in my heart a marvelous love
for the faithful ones who dwell in your land.
Those who choose other gods
increase their sorrows.

Never will I offer their offerings of blood
Never will I take their name upon my lips.

O God, it is you who are my
portion and my cup;
it is you yourself who are my prize.
The lot marked out for me is my delight;
welcome indeed the heritage that falls
to me!

I will bless you, for you give me counsel,
even at night your direct my heart.
I am always aware of your presence.
You are at my side; / I shall stand firm.

And so my heart rejoices, I sing for joy;
my body shall rest in safety.
For you will not leave me among the dead
nor let your beloved know decay.

You will show me the path of life,
the fullness of joy in your presence.
You will be my happiness forever.

Reading

O God, you are my life. I will honor you,
praising your name, for you are faithful and
true. Therefore a strong people will honor you;
nations will hold you in awe. You are a refuge to
the poor, a refuge to the needy in distress,
shelter from the rain, shade from the heat.

(Isaiah 25:1, 3-4)

Reflection

As God's Word unfolds
it gives shelter.

Prayer

God, hear the prayer of your faithful for you
are ever gracious to your people.

WEDNESDAY

Morning

Call to Prayer
I reverence God
for whom I long.

Antiphon
My strength and my courage
come from you, O God.

Psalm 42
Like a deer that yearns for running streams,
so my soul is yearning for God.

My soul is thirsting for God,
the God of my life;
when can I enter and see the face of God?

My tears have become my food,
by night, by day, as I hear it said
all day long, "Where is your God?"

These things will I remember
as I pour out my soul:
how I would lead the rejoicing crowd
    into the house of God,

amid cries of gladness and thanksgiving,
with the multitude keeping festival.

Why are you cast down, my soul?
Why groan within me?
Put your hope in God.
I will still cherish God.

My soul is cast down within me
    as I think of you,
in the land of Jordan and Mount Hermon,
on the Hill of Mizar.

Deep calls unto deep
in the roar of mighty waters;
your torrents and all your waves
    rush over me.

By day God bestows loving kindness;
by night I sing a hymn in praise
    of the living God.

I will say to God, my rock,
"Why have you forgotten me?
Why must I go mourning,
oppressed by the foe?"

With cries that pierce me to the heart
my enemies revile me,
saying to me all day long,
"Where is your God?"

Why are you cast down, my soul?
Why groan within me?
Put your hope in God.
I will still cherish God.

Reading

I declare and solemnly attest in Christ Jesus;
you must lay aside your former way of life and
the old self which deteriorates through illusion
and desire, and acquire a fresh, spiritual way of
thinking. You must put on that new person
created in God's image, whose justice and holiness are born in truth. (Ephesians 4:17a, 22-24)

Reflection

As God's Word unfolds
it gives answer.

Prayer

God, source of strength, give courage to
those who know your name and bless all
people with peace.

Evening

Call to Prayer

I reverence God
who gives me rest.

Antiphon

In God is my safety and glory.

Psalm 62

In God alone I am at rest;
my help comes from the Holy One.
I shall not be disturbed;
I stand firm.

How long will the wicked attack me?
They break me down as though I were
    a crumbling wall.

Their plan is only to destroy;
they take pleasure in lies.
With their mouths they utter blessings,
but in their hearts they curse.

In God alone I am at rest;
my hope comes from the Holy One.
I shall not be disturbed; I stand firm.

In God is my safety and glory,
the rock of my strength.
Take refuge in God, all you people,
trusting at all times,
pouring out your hearts in praise.

A simple breath is all we are,
whether rich or poor, great or small.

When weighed in a balance,
all will be lighter than a breath.

Do not rely on violence
or oppress the poor.
Do not set your heart on riches,
even though they may increase.

God has spoken and I have heard:
"I am the source of your strength.
All will be repaid according to their deeds."

Reading

God gives strength to the fainting; for the weak
God makes vigor abound. Though the young
faint and grow weary, and youths stagger and
fall, they that hope in God will renew their
strength, they will soar as with eagles' wings;
they will run and not grow weary, walk and not
grow faint.   (Isaiah 40:29-31)

Reflection

As God's Word unfolds
it gives strength.

Prayer

God, energize your people with renewed
hope. Grant them a restful night and
another new day.

Thursday

Morning

Call to Prayer
> I reverence God
> whose presence I seek.

Antiphon
> God will protect the footsteps of the just.
> The faithful ones will be blest.

Psalm 84
> How lovely is your dwelling place,
>   God of Life.
>
> I am longing and yearning,
> yearning for your presence.
> My whole being cries out to you,
> to you, the living God.
>
> Even the sparrows find a home,
> and the swallows a nest for their young.
> As for me, I search for you,
> O God of life, Eternal One.
>
> They who dwell in your presence
> forever sing your praise.
> The hearts of those whose strength is in you
>   are set on Zion's path.

As they go through the valley of bitterness,
they make it a place of running springs;
the early autumn rains clothe it
    with blessings.
They walk with ever growing strength;
they will see you, O God of Zion.

O God of Life, hear my prayer;
listen, O God of Israel.

Turn to us, O God, our refuge;
look on the face of your anointed.

One day within your house
is better than a thousand without you.
The threshold of your house
I prefer to the dwellings of the wicked.

You are our source of strength;
you give us your favor and glory.
You will not refuse any good
to those who walk in sincerity.

God of Life,
happy are they who trust in you!

Reading

Do not worry about your livelihood, what you are
to eat or drink or use for clothing. Is not life
more than food? Is not the body more valuable
than clothes? Seek first the reign of God over
you, God's way of holiness, and all these things
will be given you besides. Enough, then, of wor-
rying about tomorrow. Let tomorrow take
care of itself. Today has troubles enough of its
own.   (Matthew 6:25, 33-34)

Reflection

As God's Word unfolds
it gives assurance.

Prayer

God, you grant the desire of the heart and
do not refuse the prayer of the lips. Give
choice blessings to those who seek peace.

Evening

Call to Prayer

I reverence God
from whom all blessing comes.

Antiphon

A grateful heart I offer you, O God,
as I call upon your name.

Psalm 72

O God, give your judgment to your anointed
that the people may be governed with justice
and the poor with fairness.

May the mountains echo peace
and the hills justice.
May your anointed defend the poor
and save the children of the needy.
May peace endure like the sun
    and the moon, from age to age,
and descend like rain on the meadow,
like showers watering the earth.

Justice shall flourish in those days,
a profound peace from sea to sea
and to the ends of the earth,
until the moon shines no more.
Enemies shall fall,
and hate shall be no more.

The rulers of Tarshish and the coastlands
shall pay tribute.
The leaders of Sheba and Seba
shall bring gifts;
all will honor your anointed.

When the poor cry, they will be saved.
From oppression they will be rescued,
for precious are their lives.

Your anointed will intercede
and all will receive blessings.

May corn be abundant in the land
and all the fields be robed in wheat.
May fruit trees be clothed with plenty
and rustle like Lebanon cedars.
Like growing grass may all the
    cities flourish.

As long as the sun and moon give light,
may your anointed be blessed forever.
Every nation shall be blessed.
Beauty and glory rest in your name, O God.

Reading
Strive for peace with all people, and for that
holiness without which no one can see God. See
to it that no one falls away from the grace of
God; that no bitter root springs up through
which many may become defiled.
                    (Hebrews 12:14-15)

Reflection
 As God's Word unfolds
 it gives conviction.

Prayer
 God, all will receive blessing who call upon
 your name and seek to be holy as you are
 holy.

Friday

Morning

Call to Prayer
I reverence God
whose kindness is renewed each day.

Antiphon
May your love and faithfulness
protect me, O God,
so that I might always praise you.

Psalm 101
A song of justice and kindness
I sing to you, O God.
I shall walk in the way of integrity.
When, O God, will you come?

I shall walk with blameless heart
within my house;
I shall not set before my eyes
whatever is unjust.

I shall hate the ways of the oppressors;
they shall not be my friends.
The false-hearted must keep far away;
I shall walk the path of justice.

Those who slander their neighbors
 will be silenced.
Proud hearts and haughty looks
 will never endure.

I look to the faithful in the land
that they may dwell with me.
Those who walk in the way of integrity
 shall be welcomed.

No one who practices deceit,
no one who utters lies
shall live within my house.

Each morning I have resolved
that all the wicked in the land
 shall be uprooted.
Justice and kindness shall prevail.

Reading

Your thoughts should be wholly directed to all
that is true, all that deserves respect, all that is
honest, pure, admirable, decent, virtuous, or
worthy of praise. Live according to what you
have learned and accepted, what you have heard
me say and seen me do. Then will the God of
peace be with you.   (Philippians 4:8-9)

Reflection

As God's Word unfolds
 it gives encouragement.

Prayer

God, there is no just and saving God
but you. Be with those who walk
in your ways.

Evening

Call to Prayer

I reverence God
who does not fail me in my hope.

Antiphon

Uphold me, O God,
according to your Word.

Psalm 61

O God, hear my cry for help.
From the ends of the earth I call;
my spirit fails.

I pray that you make new this heart.
Lead me to a place of rest,
for you have been my refuge,
my strength against the foe.

Let me dwell in your presence forever;
hide me in the shelter of your wings.
You, O God, hear my prayer.
Grant me the heritage
    of all who honor your name.

May your love and faithfulness protect me.
so that I might always praise you
and day after day fulfill my vows.

Reading

Now that we have been justified by faith, we are
at peace with God through Jesus Christ.
Through Christ we have gained access by faith to
the grace in which we now stand, and we boast
of all afflictions! We know that affliction makes
for endurance, and endurance for tested virtue,
and tested virtue for hope. And this hope will not
leave us disappointed, because the love of God
has been poured out in our hearts.

(Romans 5:1-5)

Reflection

As God's Word enfolds
it gives hope.

Prayer

God, how great are your riches for those who
hope. Purify the intentions of those who
trust in your saving help.

Saturday

Morning

Call to Prayer
> I reverence God
> who does not abandon me.

Antiphon
> My heart is ready
> to call on you at dawn, O God.

Psalm 25
> To you, O God, I lift up my soul.
> I trust in you; let me not be disappointed;
> do not let my enemies triumph.
> Those who hope in you
> shall not be disappointed,
> but only those who heedlessly break faith.

> Your ways make known to me.
> Teach me your paths.
> Guide me in your truth, / teach me;
> for you are the God of my salvation.

> Because of your goodness
> I hope in you all day long.
> Remember, your compassion
> and your steadfast love are from of old.

Do not remember the sins of my youth.
In your love remember me.

God is good and upright,
showing the path to those who stray,
guiding the humble in the right path,
teaching the way to the poor.

God's ways are faithfulness and love
for those who keep the covenant.

For the sake of your name
forgive my guilt, for it is great.

Those who reverence God
will be shown the path of life.
They shall live in happiness,
and their children shall possess the land.

God's friendship is for the faithful;
to them the covenant is revealed.

My eyes are always on God
who rescues my feet from the snare.

Turn to me and have mercy,
for I am lonely and poor.
Relieve the distress of my heart,
free me from my sufferings.
See my affliction and my pain
and take all my sins away.

See how my enemies multiply,
how violent their hatred has grown.
Preserve my life and rescue me.
Do not disappoint me; / you are my refuge.
May truth and integrity protect me,
for my hope is in you, O God.

Redeem Israel from all its distress.

Reading
Beloved, let us love in deed and in truth and not
merely talk about it. This is our way of knowing
we are committed to the truth and are at peace
before God no matter what our consciences may
charge us with; for God is greater than our
hearts and all is known to God. Beloved, if our
consciences have nothing to charge us with, we
can be sure that God is with us and that we will
receive whatever we ask from God. Why? Because we are keeping God's commandments and
doing what is pleasing in God's sight.

(I John 3:18-22)

Reflection
As God's Word unfolds
it gives confidence.

Prayer
God, ever-faithful and loving, redeem those
who call upon you. Show your tenderness
and compassion.

SABBATH TIME

"A sanctuary in time" is what Rabbi Abraham Heschel calls the Sabbath. For Christians, the Sabbath, or God's Day, begins on Saturday evening and ends on Sunday evening. The main intent of Sabbath is to rest in God, to let go of our need to produce and to allow ourselves to be enveloped in the tent of God's peace.

Traditionally, Sabbath is observed in the Christian tradition by communal worship. In addition to this, special rituals, traditions, practices and prayers can be helpful. We might want to plan a family prayer and/or a special meal, invite friends over, take a walk, sit with nature, play, read, visit relatives or the ill or elderly. The time can include anything that enables us to be more reflective of and grateful for the gift of life.

Because Sabbath is intended to make us more aware of "holiness in time," it is a good practice to mark the beginning and ending of Sabbath. The prayers on the following pages will help us to do that.

In the Jewish tradition, the smelling of a special spice box is part of the ritual that closes the Sabbath. Inhaling the sweet fragrance is a reminder that the joy and rest of the Sabbath

must be strong enough to waft and whiff through
the other six days. In time, each moment of each
day becomes "a sanctuary in time," an everlasting sabbath.

Saturday Evening/Sabbath Vigil

Kindle the Light
May this Sabbath light
lift our spirits and lighten our hearts.

Invocation
May God bless us with Sabbath joy.
May God bless us with Sabbath holiness.
May God bless us with Sabbath peace.

Antiphon
We long for the Everlasting Sabbath,
holy day of our God, day of joy.

Psalm 121
I lift up my eyes to the mountains.
Will they give me strength?
My help shall come from you,
O Maker of heaven and earth.

Ever-watchful, you guide my steps.
Guardian of Israel, you never sleep.

You, O God, guard and shade me.
You stand at my side.
By day the sun shall not harm me
nor the moon by night.

You will guard me from evil;
you will guard my life
and watch over my coming and going,
now and forever.

Reading
The heavens and the earth were finished. On the
seventh day God finished the work which had
been done, and rested. So God blessed the
seventh day and made it holy, because on it God
rested from all the work of creation.

(Genesis 2:1-3)

Reflection
Holy One of Blessing, you summon the
mingling shadows of twilight.

Sunday/ Sabbath

Morning Prayer

Kindle the Light
>May this Sabbath light
>lift our spirits and lighten our hearts.

Invocation
>May God bless us with Sabbath joy.
>May God bless us with Sabbath holiness.
>May God bless us with Sabbath peace.

Antiphon
>We long for the Everlasting Sabbath,
>holy day of our God, day of joy.

Psalm 99
>O God, you are the source of all blessings;
>you sustain us in life itself.
>At your name,
>all peoples, all creation, stand in awe.
>
>Holy are you, O God!
>Holy is your name!
>You are the Eternal One.
>We praise your great name.
>You are holy, full of splendor and glory.

You are a God who loves justice.
You have established your judgment
    and justice in Israel.

Let us exalt God.
Stand in God's presence,
in the holy dwelling place.

You are holy.
The anointed called, and you answered,
speaking to them from within a cloud.
They heard and understood
and kept the law which you,
    the Holy One, gave them.

Though in your justice
you help them accountable,
to them you were a forgiving God.

Let us exalt God.
Let us praise this holy name forever.
Holy are you, O God! Holy is your name!

Reading
Take care to keep holy the Sabbath day as God
commanded you. Six days you may labor and
do all your work: but the seventh day is the
Sabbath of God. No work may be done by
you. For remember that you were once held
captive in Egypt, and God brought you from that

land into freedom. That is why God has commanded you to observe the Sabbath day.

(Deuteronomy 5:12-15)

Reflection

Holy One of Blessing,
you open the gates to morning.

Evening Prayer

Kindle the Light

May this Sabbath light
lift our spirits and lighten our hearts.

Invocation

May God bless us with Sabbath joy.
May God bless us with Sabbath holiness.
May God bless us with Sabbath peace.

Antiphon

We long for the Everlasting Sabbath,
holy day of our God, day of joy.

Psalm 139

O God, you search me and know me.
You know my resting and my rising;
you discern all my thoughts.
You know when I walk or lie down;
you are familiar with all my ways.

Before ever a word is on my tongue,
you know it through and through.
Your presence surrounds me;
 your blessing is ever upon me.
 Too wonderful for me, this knowledge.
 too high, beyond my reach.

Where can I go from your spirit,
 or where can I flee from your presence?
If I climb the heavens, you are there.
If I lie in the grave you are there.

If I take the wings of the dawn
and dwell at the sea's furthest end,
even there you will lead me
and hold me fast.

If I ask darkness to hide me,
this darkness is not dark for you,
and night is as bright as day.

For it was you who formed me,
knit me together in my mother's womb.
I thank you for the wonder of my being,
for the wonders of all your creation.

Already you knew me.
When I was being fashioned in the depths,
my body held no secret from you.
Before one of my days came into being,
you saw all my actions.

How mysterious your thoughts!
How endless their number!
They are more than the sands.
To count them I must be eternal like you.

Search me, God, and know my heart.
Test me and know my thoughts.
See that I follow not the wrong path
and lead me in the way of life eternal.

Reading

In days to come the dwelling of the God of Life
shall be upon the highest mountain, exalted
above the hills. All nations shall stream toward
it; many people shall come and say, "Come, let us
climb the holy mountain to the dwelling of the
Eternal One that we may be taught holy ways
and learn to walk in these paths. Instruction
shall flow from Zion, the word of the Holy One
from Jerusalem." God shall be the judge of the
nations and impose terms on all the peoples.
They shall turn their swords into plowshares
and their spears into pruning tools. One nation
shall not raise arms against another; training for
war will be no more. God alone is the source of
peace. Let us walk in the holy presence.

(Isaiah 2:2-5)

Reflection

May the light of this candle live on in us
until we greet the next Sabbath.

(Extinguish candle.)

Holy One of Blessing, you spread the shelter
of peace over us and all the world.

Midday Prayer

Mantra

> Let not the heat of the noonday sun
> wither my spirit or lay waste my hopes.
> May I be ever green,
> a strong shoot of justice,
> a steadfast tree of peace.
> — *Mary Lou Kownacki, OSB*

Antiphon

> Peace is mine; and all is well.

Psalm 119 (Peh)

> Your will is wonderful indeed;
> therefore I obey it.
> As your word unfolds, it gives light
> and teaches the simple.
>
> I open my mouth and sigh
> as I yearn for your commands.
> Turn and show me your mercy;
> show justice to your friends.
>
> Let my steps be guided by your promise;
> let no evil rule me.
> Redeem me from oppression
> and I will keep your precepts.

Let your face shine on your servant
and teach me your decrees.
Tears stream from my eyes
because your law is disobeyed.

Reading
Your life shall be brighter than the noonday; its
gloom shall become as morning, and you shall be
secure, because there is hope; you shall look
round you and lie down in safety, and you shall
take your rest with none to disturb.

(Job 11:17-19)

Reflection
As God's Word unfolds,
it gives security.

Mantra
Let not the heat of the noonday sun
wither my spirit or lay waste my hopes.
May I be ever green,
a strong shoot of justice,
a steadfast tree of peace.

— *Mary Lou Kownacki, OSB*

Night Prayer

Mantra

One more day to serve.
One more hour to love.
One more minute to praise.
For this day I am grateful.
If I awaken to the morning sun,
I am grateful.

— *Mary Lou Kownacki, OSB*

Antiphon

My soul is longing for your peace, O God.

Psalm 4

When I call, answer me, O God of Justice.
In the past you relieved me from anguish;
now have mercy and hear me!

O people, how long will your hearts
    be closed,
will you love what is futile
and seek what is false?
It is God who grants favors
and hears me whenever I call.

Stand in awe; /do not sin.
Be still; /reflect in the night.
Make justice your sacrifice and trust in God.

Many say, "What can bring us happiness?"
Show me the light of your face, O God.
The joy that you give me
is much greater than the happiness
of those who have an abundant harvest.

I will lie down in peace
and sleep comes at once,
for in you alone I rest secure.

Reading

May the God of peace make you perfect in
holiness. May God preserve you whole and
entire, spirit, soul and body, irreproachable at
the coming of Jesus Christ.

(I Thessalonians 5:23)

Reflection

As God's Word unfolds,
it gives peace.

Mantra

One more day to serve.
One more hour to love.
One more minute to praise.
For this day I am grateful.
If I awaken to the morning sun,
I am grateful.

— Mary Lou Kownacki, OSB

Praying Through
the Year

Compiled by Marilyn Schauble, OSB
and Charlotte Zalot, OSB.

Advent

Call to Prayer
In stillness I wait.

Antiphon
Justice shall flourish in God's time,
and fullness of peace forever.

Psalm 85B
I will hear what you have to say,
a voice that speaks of peace,
a peace for your chosen ones,
those who open their hearts.
Help is near for all who believe in you.
Glory will dwell in our land.

Mercy and faithfulness meet;
Justice and peace embrace.
Faithfulness springs from the earth,
and justice looks down from heaven.

God, you make us prosper
and our earth shall yield its fruit.
Justice shall walk before you
and peace shall follow your steps.

Readings

Sunday

As to the exact day or hour, no one knows it, neither the angels in the heavens nor even the Beloved, but only God. Be constantly on the watch! Stay awake! You do not know when the appointed time will come.   (Mark 13:32-33)

Monday

It is now the hour for you to wake from sleep, for our salvation is closer than when we first accepted the faith. The night is far spent; the day draws near. Let us cast off deeds of darkness and put on the armor of light.

(Romans 13:11b-12)

Tuesday

Rejoice in God always! I say it again, Rejoice! Everyone should see how unselfish you are. God is near. Dismiss all anxiety from your minds. Present your needs to God in every form of prayer and in petitions full of gratitude. Then God's own peace, which is beyond all understanding, will stand guard over your hearts and minds, in Christ Jesus.   (Philippians 4:4-7)

Wednesday

Stop passing judgment before the Day of return. God will bring to light what is hidden in darkness and manifest the intentions of hearts. At

that time, everyone will receive praise from God.
(I Corinthians 4:5)

Thursday
Be patient until the coming of Jesus Christ. See
how the farmer awaits the precious yield of the
soil, being patient with it until it receives the
winter and spring rains. You, too, must be
patient. Steady your hearts, because the coming
of Jesus Christ is at hand.   (James 5:7-8)

Friday
Everything written before our time was written
for our instruction, that we might derive hope
from the lessons of patience and the words of
encouragement in the Scriptures. May God, the
Source of all patience and encouragement,
enable you to live in perfect harmony with one
another according to the spirit of Christ Jesus, so
that with one heart and voice you may
glorify God.   (Romans 15:4-6)

Saturday
Rejoice always, never cease praying, render
constant thanks; such is God's will for you in
Christ Jesus. Do not stifle the Spirit. Do not
despise prophecies. Test everything; retain what
is good. Avoid any semblance of evil. May the
God of peace make you perfect in holiness. May
God preserve you whole and entire, spirit, soul
and body, irreproachable at the coming of Jesus

Christ. The One who calls us is trustworthy,
therefore God will do it.

(I Thessalonians 5:16-24)

Reflection
As God's Word unfolds
the Incarnate One is revealed.

Prayer
God, Awaited One, in you alone will love
and truth meet, and justice and peace
embrace. May the lives of your people
unfold this mystery.

Christmas

Call to Prayer
In peace, I rejoice.

Antiphon
God, the source of life and goodness,
has come.

Psalm 96
Sing unto God a new song.
All you earth, burst forth in praise.
Sing and bless God's holy name.

Proclaim God's help day after day;
tell among the nations this glory
and these wonders to all people.

God is great, worthy of praise,
glorious beyond all gods;
all other gods are as nothing.

It was God who made the universe
in beauty, dignity, and holiness,
with splendor in this holy place.

Give to God, you families and nations;
give of our precious gifts.
Give praise, and honor God's name.

Bring an offering and enter God's presence.
Stand in this holy place;
walk reverently, O Earth.

Proclaim to the nations / "God is eternal."
The world is made firm in its place;
the peoples will be judged in fairness.

Let the skies ring with joy;
let the fullness of the sea exult;
let the bounteous land rejoice.
All the woodland trees dance with joy
in the presence of God
who comes to govern the earth.

With justice God will govern the universe
and all peoples with truth.

Readings
Sunday
A child is born to us, a child is given us; upon
whose shoulder dominion rests. This child's gov-
ernance is vast and forever peaceful, both now
and forever.   (Isaiah 9:5a, 6)

Monday
How beautiful upon the mountains are the feet
of those who bring glad tidings, announcing salvation, and saying to Zion, "Your God is ruler
over all." Hark! Your watchers raise a cry,
together they shout for joy, for they see directly,
before their eyes, God restoring Zion. Break out
together in song, O ruins of Jerusalem! For God
comforts the people, and redeems Jerusalem. All
the ends of the earth will behold the salvation
of God.   (Isaiah 52:7-10)

Tuesday
When the designated time had come, God sent
forth Jesus Christ born of Mary, born under
the law, to deliver from the law those who were
subjected to it, so that we might receive our
status as adopted sons and daughters. The proof
that you are sons and daughters is the fact that
God has sent forth into our hearts the spirit of
Jesus Christ which cries out "Abba!" You are no

longer slaves but sons and daughters. And the fact that you are sons and daughters makes you inheritors, by God's design. (Galatians 4:4-7)

Wednesday

In the beginning was the Word; the Word was in God's presence. The Word was God and was present in the beginning. Through the Word all things came into being, and apart from the Word nothing came to be. Whatever came to be in the Word, found life, life for the light of all people. The light shines on in darkness, a darkness that did not overcome it. (John 1:1-5)

Thursday

The grace of God has appeared, offering salvation to all. It trains us to reject godless ways and worldly desires, and live temperately, justly, and devoutly in this age as we await our blessed hope, the appearing of the glory of the great God and our Savior Christ Jesus. It was Christ who sacrificed himself for us, to redeem us from all unrighteousness and to cleanse for himself a people of his own, eager to do what is right. (Titus 2:11-14)

Friday

When the kindness and love of God our savior appeared, we were saved; not because of any righteous deeds we had done, but because of

God's mercy. We were saved through the
baptism of new birth and renewal by the Holy
Spirit. This Spirit God lavished on us through
Jesus Christ our Savior, that we might be
justified by God's grace and become inheritors, in
hope, of eternal life.   (Titus 3:4-7)

Saturday

When the angels had returned to heaven, the
shepherds said to one another: "Let us go over to
Bethlehem and see this event which God has
made known to us." They went in haste and
found Mary and Joseph, and the baby lying in
the manger; once they saw, they understood
what had been told them concerning this child.
All who heard of it were astonished at the report
given them by the shepherds. Mary treasured all
these things and reflected on them in her heart.
The shepherds returned, glorifying and praising
God for all they had heard and seen in accord
with what had been told them.   (Luke 2:15-20)

Reflection

As God's Word unfolds
the Incarnate One is celebrated.

Prayer

Glory to you, O God,
and peace to all people.
You give reason for hope and for love.
May rejoicing fill our hearts.

Lent

Call to Prayer
> Into God's hands
> I commend my spirit.

Antiphon
> Keep my spirit steady and willing, O God.

Psalm 51
> Have mercy on me, O God, in your kindness;
> in your great tenderness
>   wipe away my faults.
> Wash away my sin;
> cleanse me of my guilt.
>
> For I am well aware of my faults;
> they are always before me.
> Against you, you alone, have I sinned;
> I have done what is evil.
> You are just when you pass
>   sentence on me,
> blameless when you give judgment.
>
> You love those who search for truth.
> In wisdom, center me,
> for you know my frailty.
> With fresh flowing water
> wash me of my iniquities.

I have been brought low by my sins.
Wipe away my guilt
that I may hear the sounds
    of joy and gladness.
A clean heart create for me, O God.
Put a steadfast spirit within me.

Dismiss me not from your presence;
do not deprive me of your spirit.
Renew my joy;
a willing spirit sustain in me.
Then I shall witness to your ways
that sinners may return to you.

Free me from death,
and I will acclaim your goodness.
O God, open my lips,
and my mouth shall declare your praise.

If my heart is not sincere,
no sacrifice will be acceptable.
Your wish is for a contrite spirit.

In your kindness be bountiful to Zion.
Sacrifice will once again be pleasing to you.

Readings

Sunday

Brothers and sisters, I beg you through the
mercy of God to offer your bodies as a living
sacrifice holy and acceptable to God, your spiri-

tual worship. Do not conform yourselves to this age but be transformed by the renewal of your mind, so that you may judge what is God's will, what is good, pleasing and perfect.

(Romans 12:1-2)

Monday

Now, says God, return to me with your whole heart, with fasting, and weeping, and mourning; rend your hearts, not your garments, and return to God. For gracious and merciful is God, slow to anger, rich in kindness, and relenting in punishment   (Joel 2:12-13)

Tuesday

My friends, what good is it to profess faith without practicing it? Such faith has no power to save one, has it? If a brother or sister has nothing to wear and no food for the day, and you say to them, "Good-bye and good luck! Keep warm and well fed," but do not meet their bodily needs, what good is that? So it is with the faith that does nothing in practice. It is thoroughly lifeless.

(James 2:14-17)

Wednesday

Submit to God; resist the evil one and the evil one will take flight. Draw close to God, and God will draw close to you. Cleanse your hands, you sinners; purify your hearts, you backsliders. Begin to lament, to mourn, and to weep; let your laughter be turned into mourning and your joy into sorrow. Be humbled in the sight of God and God will raise you on high.   (James 4:7-10)

Thursday
Never be ashamed of your testimony to Christ Jesus, nor of me, a prisoner for his sake; but with the strength which comes from God bear your share of the hardship which the Gospel entails. God has saved us and has called us to a holy life, not because of any merit of ours but according to the divine plan — the grace held out to us in Christ Jesus before the world began but now made manifest through the appearance of our Savior. Jesus Christ has robbed death of its power and has brought life and immortality into clear light through the Gospel.
(II Timothy 1:8-10)

Friday
We have our citizenship in the heavens; it is from there that we eagerly await the coming of our Savior, Jesus Christ. He will give a new form to this lowly body of ours and remake it according to the pattern of his glorified body, by Christ's power to subject everything to himself. For these reasons, my friends, you whom I so love and long for, you who are my joy and my glory, continue to stand firm in faith.   (Philippians 3:20-4:1)

Saturday

In the days when Christ was in the flesh, he offered prayers and supplications with loud cries and tears to God, who was able to save him from death, and Christ was heard because of his reverence. God though he was, Christ learned obedience from what he suffered; and when perfected, he became the source of eternal salvation for all who obey him. (Hebrews 5:7-9)

Reflection

As God's Word unfolds
mercy is made manifest.

Prayer

Save your people, O God.
Re-create hearts of faith and courage,
constancy and peace,
hearts that are simple and free.

Easter

Call to Prayer

I know that my Redeemer lives.
I have reason to rejoice.

Antiphon

This is the day that God has made;
I rejoice and am glad!

Psalm 30

I will praise you, God,
for you have rescued me;
you did not let my enemies rejoice over me.

I cried to you for help,and you healed me.
You raised me from the dead.
I was with those in the depths,
but you restored my life.

Sing psalms to God, all you faithful ones;
give thanks.

God's anger lasts a moment;
God's favor, a lifetime.
At night there are tears;
at dawn, rejoicing.

In good times, I thought
that I would never be disturbed,
that my good fortune would remain.
With honor you had favored me,
but I did not feel your presence,
and so I was filled with fear.

I cried aloud to you,
"What profit would my death be?
Can dust give you praise
or proclaim your faithfulness?"

You changed my mourning into dancing;
you removed my sackcloth
and clothed me with joy.
I shall not cease to praise you,
giving thanks forever.

Readings
Sunday
God raised him from the dead, and for many
days thereafter Jesus appeared to those who had
come up with him from Galilee to Jerusalem.
These are the witnesses now before the people.
We ourselves announce to you the good news
that what God promised our ancestors has been
fulfilled for us in raising up Jesus, according to
what is written in the second psalm, "You are
mine; this day I have begotten you."

(Acts 13:30-33)

Monday
If we have died with Christ, we believe that we
are also to live with Christ. We know that
Christ, once raised from the dead, will never die
again; death has no more power over him.
Christ's death was death to sin, once for all;
Christ's life is life for God. In the same way, you
must consider yourselves dead to sin but alive
for God in Christ Jesus.   (Romans 6:8-11)

Tuesday

If Christ is in you, the body is dead because of sin, while the spirit lives because of justice. If the Spirit of God who raised Christ from the dead dwells in you, then God who raised Christ from the dead will bring your mortal bodies to life also, through Christ's Spirit dwelling in you.

(Romans 8:10-11)

Wednesday

We do not live for ourselves alone, nor do we die for ourselves alone. While we live we are responsible to God, and when we die we die as God's servants. Both in life and in death we are God's. That is why Christ died and came to life again, that he might be God of both the dead and the living.   (Romans 14:7-9)

Thursday

Beloved, let us love in deed and in truth and not merely talk about it. This is our way of knowing we are committed to the truth and are at peace before God no matter what our consciences may charge us with; for God is greater than our hearts and all is known to God.

(I John 3:18-20)

Friday

They killed him finally, hanging him on a tree, only to have God raise him up on the third day and grant that he be seen, not by all, but only by

such witnesses as had been chosen beforehand
by God — by us who ate and drank with him
after he rose from the dead. Christ commissioned
us to preach to the people and to bear witness
that he is the One set apart by God as judge of
the living and the dead. To him all the prophets
testify, saying that everyone who believes in him
has forgiveness of sin through his name.

(Acts 10:40-43)

Saturday

Praised be the God of Jesus Christ, who in great
mercy gave us new birth; a birth unto hope
which draws its life from the resurrection of
Jesus Christ from the dead; a birth to an
i;mperishable inheritance, incapable of fading or
defilement, which is kept in the heavens for you
who are guarded with God's power through faith;
a birth to a salvation which stands ready to be
revealed in the last days. There is cause for
rejoicing here. You may for a time have to suffer
the distress of many trials: but this is so that
your faith, which is more precious than the
passing splendor of fire-tried gold, may by its
genuineness lead to praise, glory, and honor
when Jesus Christ appears.   (I Peter 1:3-7)

Reflection

As God's Word unfolds
Resurrection is understood.

Prayer

God of Everlasting life, the peace of your
presence embraces all in the joy of Resurrection. To you be glory forever! Alleluia!

Mary,
Wellspring of Peace

PRAYERS

Mary, Queen of Peace,
We entrust our lives to you.
Shelter us from war, hatred
and oppression.

Teach us
to live in peace,
to educate ourselves for peace.

Inspire us to act justly,
to revere all God has made.

Root peace firmly in our hearts
and in our world.

Amen.

— Pope John Paul II

Hail Mary

Hail Mary, full of grace, God is with you. Blessed
are you among women and blessed is the fruit of
your womb, Jesus. Holy Mary, Mother of God,
pray for us sinners, now and at the hour of our
death. Amen.

The circle of a girl's arms
has changed the world,
the round, sorrowful world,
to a cradle for God.
O Mother of God,
be hands that are rocking the world
to a kind rhythm of love:
that the incoherence of war
and the chaos of unrest
be soothed to a lullaby,
and the round, sorrowful world,
in your hands,
the cradle of God.

— *Caryll Houselander*

Prayer to Our Lady of the Americas

Virgin of hope, Mother of the poor,
Our Lady of Pilgrims,
today we pray to you for our race and continent,
the land you visit with bare feet,
offering the riches of the Child
held tightly in your arms,
a fragile child who makes us rich,
an enslaved child who makes us free,
Virgin of Hope.

Upon the peoples who walked in darkness
has shone a great light.
This light is the Savior that you gave us
a long time ago in Bethlehem at midnight.
We want to walk in hope.

You know poverty and have lived it.
Give us the spirit of the poor in order to be
happy,
but alleviate the misery of our bodies
and uproot from the hearts of so many people
the egoism that impoverishes.

Our Lady of Pilgrims,
we are the people of God in America.

We are the church in pilgrimage toward Easter.
May the bishops have the hearts of fathers.
May the priests be friends of God to the people.
May the religious manifest the anticipated joy of
the reign of God.
May the lay people give witness to the Risen
Christ in their lives.
And may we walk together with all people
sharing their sufferings and hopes.

May the people
of North and South America
grow together
in the ways of peace and justice.

Our Lady of the Americas,
brighten our hopes,
lighten our poverty,
join us in the pilgrimage to God.
So be it. Amen.

— *Maryknoll Fathers and Brothers*

The Lord's promise is that he is in our midst when we gather in prayer. Strengthened by this conviction, we beseech the risen Christ to fill the world with his peace. We call upon Mary, the first disciple and the Queen of Peace, to intercede for us and for the people of our time that we may walk in the way of peace.

> — *The Challenge of Peace*
> *Pastoral Letter, US Catholic Conference*

Mary, bridge of peace, guide to pilgrims, inspiration to poets, comfort to the oppressed, light to those who wander in darkness, we praise you and ask to be one with you. United with you, we will be one with God, making peace with every person of the globe. United with you, we too will feel the mystery of Christ's peace, alive within us. Holy Mary, mother of God, pray with us. Amen.

> — *Edward Hays*

A Modern Hail Mary

Hail Mary, full of grace
give us a sense of the fullness of God
in our own lives.
Because Jesus was with you
all women are full of graces
too long denied, too long undeveloped.
Blessed are you as a woman.
Without you the Incarnation
would never have been possible.
Holy Mary, Mother of God, pray for us
so that Jesus may be seen in the women of our
day now and for all eternity. Amen.

— Joan Chittister, OSB

Hail, Holy Queen

Hail, Holy Queen, mother of mercy,
our life, our sweetness and our hope.
To you do we cry,
poor banished children of Eve;
to you do we send up our sighs,
mourning and weeping
in this valley of tears.
Turn then, most gracious advocate,
your eyes of mercy upon us,
and after this, our exile,
show unto us
the blessed fruit of your womb, Jesus.
O clement, O loving, O sweet Virgin Mary.

Prayer to Mary for the Sick

Mary, health of the sick,

Be at the bedside of all the world's sick people;
    of those who are unconscious and dying;
    of those who have begun their agony;
    of those who have abandoned all hope
        of a cure;
    of those who weep and cry out in pain:
    of those who cannot receive care
    because they have no money;
    of those who ought to be resting
    but are forced by poverty to work;
    of those who seek vainly in their beds
    for a less painful position;
    of those who pass long nights sleepless;
    of those who are tormented
    by the cares of a family in distress;
    of those who must renounce
    their most cherished plans for the future;
    of those, above all,
    who do not believe in a better life;
    of those who rebel and curse God;
    of those who do not know that Christ
    suffered like them and for them.

— Rabboni

Mary, Spark of Light,
whose faith enkindles ours,
pray for us.

Mary, Center of Compassion,
where we find the God
whose love empowers us,
pray for us.

Mary, Leaven of Life,
in whose words we hear
that God is on the side of the poor,
pray for us.

—Mary Evelyn Jegen, SND

Magnificat

I sing your praises, God with all my heart.
And I rejoice in you, O God of Life,
for you have looked upon my lowliness.
And who am I to merit your attention?

I henceforth regard myself as happy,
because you have done great things for me.
And every generation gives assent,
for you are God and your name is holy.

You give your grace anew in every age
to those who live in reverence all their lives.
Grace is your strength but you unmask all pride.
You strip us bare of our self conceit.

Dethroned are those who hold authority,
the poor and humble people you uphold.
You give in great abundance to the hungry
and send the rich away with empty hands.

Your people Israel have been remembered,
for mercy has been sent to all the faithful,
just as you promised to those before us,
to Abraham, to Sarah, their children forever.

Luke 1:46-55

— *translated by Mary David Callahan, OSB*

LITANIES

Litany of Mary of Nazareth

Glory to you, God our Creator ... Breathe into us new life, new meaning.
Glory to you, God our Savior ... Lead us in the way of peace and justice.
Glory to you, God, healing Spirit ... Transform us to empower others.

Mary, wellspring of peace .... Be our guide.
Model of strength
Model of gentleness
Model of trust
Model of courage
Model of patience
Model of risk
Model of openness
Model of perseverance

Mother of the liberator .... Pray for us.
Mother of the homeless
Mother of the dying
Mother of the nonviolent
Widowed mother
Unwed mother

Mother of a political prisoner
Mother of the condemned
Mother of an executed criminal

Oppressed woman .... Lead us to life.
Liberator of the oppressed
Marginalized woman
Comforter of the afflicted
Cause of our joy
Sign of contradiction
Breaker of bondage
Political refugee
Seeker of sanctuary
First disciple
Sharer in Christ's ministry
Participant in Christ's passion
Seeker of God's will
Witness to Christ's resurrection

Woman of mercy .... Empower us.
Woman of faith
Woman of contemplation
Woman of vision
Woman of wisdom and understanding
Woman of grace and truth
Woman, pregnant with hope
Woman, centered in God

Mary, Queen of Peace, we entrust our lives to you. Shelter us from war, hatred and oppression.
Teach us to live in peace, to educate ourselves for peace.
Inspire us to act justly, to revere all God has made.
Root peace firmly in our hearts and in our world.
Amen.

— *Pax Christi USA*

Litany of Mary, Bridge of Peace

Madonna of the Globe ....
> *Mary our hope, Mary our joy,*
> *hear our prayer.*

Mother of Prophets
Mother of the Homeless
Our Lady of Vladimir
Refuge of Families
Model of Courage
Madre del Pueblo
Liberator of the Oppressed
Our Lady of the Missions
Star of the Sea
Queen of Peace
Mother of the Dying
Our Lady of Guadalupe
Model of Trust
Mother of the Disappeared

Fugitive in Egypt
Our Lady of Kazan
Beloved of God
Our Lady of Czestochowa
Cause of Our Joy
Advocate of Peace
Model of Strength
Mother of the Streets
Our Lady of Lebanon
Mother of the Nonviolent
Mother of Martyrs
Mary of Nazareth
Mother of Comfort
Our Lady of Snows
Mother of the Stranger
Timeless One

— Pax Christi USA

For the Conversion of the Country

We come to you, Mary, patroness
        of the United States,
    to pray for true conversion of heart
        for our country.

We are a people who has created a society
    at war with itself.

We say we want peace; yet we use guns to
    settle our public and private disputes.

Mary, convert us to peace.

We say we want unity; yet we are deeply
    divided along racial and ethnic lines.

Mary, convert us to unity.

We say we want to restore family values;
        yet divorce,
    drugs, promiscuity and abortion continually
        tear apart family bonds.

Mary, convert us to wholeness of heart.

We say we are concerned about the poor
 and homeless among us; yet we set aside
  billions for a defense budget
   of staggering proportions.

Mary, convert us to compassion.

Take our hopes, Mary, to the heart of your Son.
Strengthened by your intercession, we dare to
hope that conversion of heart is possible for each
of us and all of us. Amen.

   — Stephanie Campbell, OSB

ROSARY

The rosary is one of the oldest and most popular forms of prayer in the Catholic Church. It has nourished countless generations from popes to assembly line workers to grade school children.

Bishop Thomas Gumbleton, the founding president of Pax Christi USA, prays a rosary each day before going to bed. "Daily recitation of the rosary provides the slower, more meditative rhythm needed to counteract the multiple pressures of our busy lives," he said. "The rosary empowers me to slow down, re-focus and re-dedicate my activities and thoughts to Gospel principles."

When praying the rosary, we focus on significant events in the life of Jesus and Mary. These events are divided into the Joyful Mysteries, the Sorrowful Mysteries, and the Glorious Mysteries.

Immersing ourselves in the lives of Jesus and Mary while slowly and mindfully repeating the Our Father and Hail Mary has the power to transform us. The physical act of keeping track of prayers while holding beads helps us to concentrate. While the external senses are anchored and centered, the mind is freer to enter more deeply into the heart of God.

The Sign of the Cross and
The Apostles' Creed

The Our Father

Three Hail Marys

Glory Be...

The Our Father

Glory Be...

(First Mystery)

(Fifth Mystery)

Ten Hail Marys

Ten Hail Marys

The Our Father

Glory Be to the Father

Glory Be...

The Our Father

(Fourth Mystery)

(Second Mystery)

Ten Hail Marys

Ten Hail Marys

The Our Father

Glory Be...

Glory Be...

The Our Father

Ten Hail Marys

(Third Mystery)

This is an abridged version of *In Pursuit of Peace:
Praying the Rosary Through the Psalms,* by Joan
Chittister, OSB.

The unabridged book may be obtained from Pax
Christi USA.

The Joyful Mysteries

The Annunciation

"Behold the handmaid of the Lord, be it done unto me according to your word." Lk. 1:38

The words of Mary trip so lightly off the tongue, until our moment of annunciation comes, until God invites us to do things we don't want to do. God's annunciation to us is, "Sell what you have and give to the poor" — here in our own cities where we keep the poor carefully hidden behind the welfare agencies. God announces, "Love one another" — even the people our country is teaching us to hate. God announces, "Do unto others what you would have others do unto you" — and we hear that word in a culture that puts more money into the military than it does into food, education and housing. Where do we turn for strength when we hear all that? We can turn to Mary, the young woman who knew that if she listened to the unconventional call of God to accept the unexpected, unexplainable child, she stood to lose it all — her honor in the community, her future security, her marriage. But Mary trusted that God's will was more to be followed than her own. Whatever the cost.

The Visitation

"When Elizabeth heard Mary's greeting, the baby stirred in her womb." Lk. 1:40

Elizabeth, the barren old woman about to have a first child, is Mary's concern. But Mary, betrothed but not married, innocent but subject to Jewish laws for adultery, young but given great responsibility, was Elizabeth's concern as well. Both are surely full of tension for themselves but no less compassionate for others. Each of these strong women, alone in her own circumstances, but steeped in the limitless love of God, reached out to give hope to the other.

Hope is a virtue without which life comes up bleak and barren. It takes hope to carry on in confusion. It takes hope to assume that God is present even when we cannot see the road ahead. It takes hope to trust that if we just keep doing what we must do for others, even in the midst of our own emotional chaos, that the God who leads us into darkness will also lead us out of it. Indeed, Mary is a model of hope for us when we would become totally consumed with ourselves.

The Nativity

*"She wrapped him in swaddling clothes and laid
him in the manger because there was no room in
the inn." Lk. 2:7*

There are times and places in life when God
seems like a very powerless companion indeed.
In the death camps in Germany, God was surely
present but depressingly silent. In times of
public rejection, God may indeed be with us but
the darkness is no less dark. In times when we
are the only ones to witness against public sin or
private corruption, the "fortress" that is God
feels mighty defenseless indeed.

The one place, perhaps, that is sure proof of
the seed of God in every bleak field of life is in
Bethlehem at the Nativity of Jesus. Where Mary
could have seen only darkness — the long trip,
the hard circumstances, the undignified sur-
roundings, the lack of family and friends — she
brought the light of faith. Where danger was
palpable around them, the serenity of faith
smothered fear because Mary opened herself to
believe that what God had begun in her, God
would bring to fullness.

The Presentation

*"You see this child ... he is destined ... to be a
sign that is rejected — and a sword will pierce*

your own soul, too." Lk. 2:35

When Mary took Jesus to present him at the temple and dedicated him to the work of God, it was she as well who was singled out for consideration. The prophet Simeon warns her that behaviors have consequences. Those who take on the life of Jesus will themselves suffer the costs of such a step. When Mary offers Jesus in the temple then, she is just as surely offering herself. And she does it with fortitude and forbearance as a sign to all of us that self-giving is not something that is done in a moment, in a single act, in a flash of mind devoid of echoes throughout life.

In the Presentation, Mary teaches us that the Christ-life, once begun, must determine every moment of our lives.

The Finding in the Temple

"My son, why have you treated us like this? Your father and I have been searching for you in great anxiety." Lk. 2:48

What is difficult is not always bad. The question is what gets us through the trauma when loss or tragedy happen? The answer, at least in part involves seeing more clearly the implications of the Finding in the Temple.

On one of the holy days, at the time of a regular Jewish festival, when people were returning to their homes together from the Temple in Jerusalem, the normalcy of life is suddenly shattered for Mary and Joseph again. The child is missing. The searching must certainly have been hectic. No one searches for a lost child in a casual way. But when they finally find him, seated in the midst of the rabbis and teaching the teachers, they realize with terrible awareness that life has something new in store for them. Something which, like us, they do not understand but must learn to trust.

The Sorrowful Mysteries

The Agony in the Garden

"If it be your will, take this cup away from me. Yet not my will but yours be done." Lk. 22:42

What can possibly be a healthy response to the irrational, the unexplainable, the unacceptable in life?

Jesus in the Garden embodies both the questions and the answer.

It is only honest to wish some things in life away. But when they do not go, when there is no way whatsoever to avoid them, then they must be borne knowing that God's will is better for us than our will for us can ever be. We would will to stay spiritual children. God wills us to grow up. We would will to have life be a perpetual sandbox. God wills life to be a mountain-climbing moment of rhapsody and accomplishment. We would will life to be a walk on velvet waters. God wills life to be a journey through four seasons, every climate, all the topographies of the soul so that when we have finished it, we can say that we have truly lived it. Well. Whole. With integrity.

The Scourging at the Pillar

"Pilate, in his desire to satisfy the mob, released Barabbas to them; and he had Jesus flogged and handed him over to be crucified." Mk. 15:15

The Scourging at the Pillar is not about blind abuse, though certainly there is plenty of that in the actions of the state that inflicts it. The Scourging at the Pillar is about not giving up when there is no apparent reason to go on. The synagogue that Jesus came to perfect has turned against him. The state that Jesus has honored fails to defend him. The people whom Jesus served have abandoned him and the disciples whom Jesus loved have denied him. There is nothing left of the dream and the destination. But Jesus goes on. He does not change his mind. He does not give in. He does not quit. He simply, silently, and stolidly persists, despite the abuse, the abandonment, the death of the dream.

Jesus scourged is a model of a passion that never dies.

The Crowning with Thorns

"The soldiers dressed him in purple, and plaiting a crown of thorns, placed it on his head." Mk. 15:17

To withstand gloating and shame is no small miracle of life. It was the ability to live through shame and gloating that made the first interracial marriages possible. It was the courage to live through shame and gloating that made the first anti-war protests conceivable. It is the grace to live through shame and gloating that makes spiritual adulthood thinkable at all.

But from what well can we draw the steadfastness it takes to be different, to be other, to be left out, to be singular in a society that wants conformity without question. Jesus at the Crowning with Thorns—jeered at by soldiers, toyed with by underlyings, humiliated by agents of a conformist society — stood stark-still in the face of gloating. Jesus, mocked, teased, derided and ridiculed waits for us to find something in life for which we would be willing to become a public joke.

The Carrying of the Cross

"As they led him away to execution they seized upon a man called Simon, from Cyrene, on his way in from the country, put the cross on his back, and made him walk behind Jesus carrying it." Lk. 23:26

To be tested, to be tried is to bring to the cold eye of judgment everything we have ever said we are and have never had to prove. To be tested is to begin with Jesus the long, slow, lonely climb to Calvary where helpers are few and supporters are weak and the setbacks are many.

The following of Jesus to Calvary demands that we carry the cross of human responsibility, of human justice. The following of Jesus to Calvary demands that we carry those who cannot carry themselves through life; that we carry and carry until every child in the world who needs to be borne to life has been carried across the seas of poverty and abuse and destruction. The following of Jesus to Calvary means that we do not fail the test to become human, human beings who, in the center of the demonic, live for the will of God alone.

The Crucifixion and Death of Jesus

"Then Jesus gave a loud cry and said, 'Father, into your hands I commit my spirit'; and with these words he died." Lk. 23:46

Is there anything worth giving our lives for or is life simply a series of events that come and go with no overreaching value in them?

It is to the crucifixion that we look for that model of total commitment that demands that we take a stand on behalf of the human race. The fearful apostles were surely not worth dying for, but Jesus did. The generations to come, you and I and our cowering selves were surely not worth dying for, but Jesus did.

It is to the crucifixion that we look to measure the authenticity and measure of our own life value. The point is not that we should die for something; the point is simply that we should be fearless enough to be willing to give our lives for something bigger than ourselves because, like Jesus, we know that Yahweh is with us and no harm can harm us nearly as much as meaninglessness can.

The Glorious Mysteries

The Resurrection

"On Sunday morning very early the women came to the tomb bringing the spices they had prepared. Finding that the stone had been rolled away from the tomb, they went inside; but the body was not be be found." Lk. 24:1-3

In every life something good fails, something great ends, something righteous is taken unjustly away, something looms like an abandonment by God. The temptation, of course, is the same for us as it was for the women in the garden: to give ourselves over to tending our tombs rather than to expect to find new life there.

But that is exactly when we must remember the Jesus of the Cross who rose from the dead as sign to us that every little death died for some good reason is life become new all over again. Everyone rises over and over again in anticipation of that moment when the last resurrection comes and the light never dims again.

The Jesus of the Resurrection stands as stark, illumined sign that life is a process of dying and rising that someday will bring us all to wholeness, if we only allow it.

The Ascension of Jesus Into Heaven

"...Why stand there looking up into the sky?"
Acts 1:11

The Ascension reminds generation after generation to raise our sights above the narrow limits of our private lives to see the design of God painted with broader stroke. It is not so much what God does in our life that is the sign of God with us. It is what God calls us to do in the lives of others that is the measure of God's continuing care. Jesus did not leave the apostles because he no longer cared for them; Jesus ascended into heaven so that, rooted in His life, the apostles might begin to care for others. Everywhere. Always. With total commitment.

The message is plain: He is not here, and there is much to be done that is far beyond our private agendas, our personal inclinations. The gospel is unfinished. The work is undone. The witness is still wanting. And there is no one left to give it now but us.

The Descent of the Holy Spirit

"And there appeared to them tongues like flames of fire, dispersed among them and resting on each one. And they were filled with the Holy Spirit. . . ." Acts 2:3, 4

Clearly we have not "been left orphans." The Holy Spirit has indeed come. The only condition of the Presence is that we allow ourselves to see the compelling reality of it, that we do not take God for granted.

Hildegard of Bingen wrote, "I am a feather on the breath of God." We, on the other hand, wrestle with life intent on wrenching everything in it into the puny and the obvious and the controllable. We refuse to let go. We plan. We strategize. We fix. We refuse to fall trustingly into the arms of the Spirit.

The Descent of the Holy Spirit is the call to be abandoned to the Will of God. It is a call to risk the consequences of God's love, here and now.

The Assumption of Mary

"So it is with the resurrection of the dead. What is sown in the earth as a perishable thing is raised imperishable. Sown in humiliation, it is raised in glory; sown in weakness it is raised in power. . . ."
1 Cor. 15:42

When we raise our hearts and souls to God, the things that drag us down will lose their grip on us. When we refuse to become imprisoned by things and status and ambition and self and greed, our souls are set free and our bodies are unburdened.

But where can we possibly go to find someone whose life is not tethered to the earth to the point of death? What proof do we have that anyone can rise above what we want, to what we can become? Mary of the Assumption teaches us to keep our eyes on the things of heaven, to free ourselves from the fetters of anything lesser, to develop a vision outside of ourselves, to allow ourselves to be lifted up beyond the petty and the transient to the eternal and the unalloyed. Mary of the Assumption is a sign of what we can become if we are willing to let go of what we have planned for ourselves.

The Coronation of Mary

"Next appeared a great portent in heaven, a woman robed with the sun, beneath her feet the moon, and on her head a crown of twelve stars." Rev. 12:1

If the Coronation of Mary says anything at all, it says that if the world calls the weak unwanted, the poor lesser, the forgotten inferior, the world is wrong. And God has used the weakest of the weak, a woman, to prove it.

The woman who turned God into the body and blood of Christ is here raised to the feminine counterpoint of the Divine. Where do women belong? At the right hand of God, obviously. Where do women belong? In the highest places of heaven, obviously. What are women called to do? The complete will of God, obviously. What are women called to be then? Images of God, obviously.

As long as any woman anywhere is denied access to God, or status in life, or equality with men, or respect and position, then Mary's place in heaven is mocked.

Litanies

A Litany of Peacemakers

God, creator of the universe, author of our covenant of peace,
we pray to you: empower us.
God, redeemer of the world, our way of peace,
we pray to you: empower us.
God, sanctifier of conscience, gift of peace,
we pray to you: empower us.
Mary, wellspring of reconciliation, mother of peacemakers, *pray for us.*
Michael, our defender in the spiritual battle with forces of our own self-destruction,
pray for us.
Heavenly hosts, angelic warriors for universal peace, ...
Moses and Miriam, nonviolent liberators, architects and singers of the covenant of justice, ...
Isaiah, critic of militarism, prophet of peace, ...
Esther, intercessor for the powerless, emissary of peace, ...
Amos and Micah and Hosea, voices for the oppressed, ...
Jeremiah, doomsday seer,
voice of lamentation, ...
Magdalene, faithful witness of Christ's execution, first witness of his resurrection, ...
Peter and Paul, prisoners of conscience, ...

Matthew, Mark, Luke, John, evangelists of the
peaceable kingdom, ...

Felicity and Perpetua, midwives and mothers,
sacrificed in the sport of a military
empire, ...

Martin of Tours, conscientious objector, ...

Francis of Assisi, lover of creation, poor man
with nothing to fight for, ...

Clare of Assisi, pacifier of armies with the power
of the Eucharist, ...

Catherine of Siena, mystic diplomat, skilled
negotiator, ...

Hildegard of Bingen, mystic, lover of Creation,

Gandhi, the Mahatma, nonviolent warrior, ...

Franz Jägerstätter, resister for Christ, ...

Simone Weil, patroness of solidarity with the
oppressed, fasting unto death with the
hungry, ...

Martin Luther King, prophet and dreamer of
the Beloved Community, ...

Thomas Merton, contemplative critic, mentor of
peacemakers, ...

Pope John XXIII, herald of peace, ...

Pope Paul VI, apostle and teacher of peace, ...

Dorothy Day, lady poverty, mother courage,
witness to the radical gospel of peace, ...

Oscar Romero, shepherd of the poor, martyr for
justice, ...

Maura, Ita, Jean, Dorothy, martyrs for the
poor, handmaids of justice, ...

Saints of the Shaker, Mennonite, Quaker, and

Church of the Brethren communions, ...
Children of light, transfigured in the fire-storms
    of Hiroshima/Nagasaki, ...
Children of darkness, transfigured in the night
    of torture and disappearance, ...
All you holy peacemakers, living and more
    living, ...
Jesus, Messiah, Prince of Peace,
    we pray to you: empower us.

— *Kathleen Deignan, CNC*

Litany for Peace

Let us pray to Jesus Christ that we may be set
free from the chains of violence and war.

Jesus the Christ, by your cross and resurrection
... *deliver us by your suffering and forgiveness*
by your nonviolence and love
by your witness to truth
by your passion and death
by your victory over the grave

from the desire for power
from the conspiracy of silence
from the negation of life
from the worship of weapons

from the celebration of killing
from the slaughter of the innocent
from the extermination of the weak
from the nightmare of hunger
from the politics of terror
from a false peace
from relying on weapons
from the spiral of armaments
from plundering the earth's resources
from the despair of this age
from global suicide.

by the light of the Gospel ... give us peace
by the good news for the poor
by your healing and wounds
by faith in your word
by a hunger and thirst for justice
by the coming of Your reign
by the outpouring of the Spirit
by reconciliation of enemies
by gentleness and nonviolence
by the truth that sets us free
by prophecy and witness
by persecution because of your name
by the power of love

Lamb of God who takes away the sins
of the world, have mercy on us

Lamb of God who takes away the sins
of the world, have mercy on us

Lamb of God who takes away the sins
of the world, grant us peace

— *Linda Friern, Tony Bartlett*

A Buddhist Litany for Peace

As we gather together, praying for peace, let us
be truly with each other.
Silence
Let us pay attention to our breathing.
Silence
Let us be relaxed in our bodies and our minds.
Silence
Let us be at peace with our bodies and our
minds.
Silence
Let us return to ourselves and become wholly
ourselves. Let us maintain a half-smile on our
faces.
Silence
Let us be aware of the source of being common to
us all and to all living things.
Silence
Evoking the presence of the Great Compassion,
let us fill our hearts with our own compassion —
towards ourselves and towards all living beings.
Silence

Let us pray that all living things realize that
they are all brothers and sisters, all nourished
from the same source of life.

Silence

Let us pray that we ourselves cease to be the
cause of suffering to each other.

Silence

Let us plead with ourselves to live in a way
which will not deprive other living beings of air,
water, food, shelter, or the chance to live.

Silence

With humility, with awareness of the existence
of life, and of the sufferings that are going on
around us, let us pray for the establishment of
peace in our hearts and on earth.

Amen.

— *Thich Nhat Hanh*

Litany of Repentance

We ask forgiveness for our complicity in the
violence now unleashed in our world and we
repent of the violence in our own hearts.

For hardness of heart .... *forgive us, we pray.*
For wasting our gifts
For wanting too much
For wounding the earth

For ignoring the poor
For trusting in weapons
For refusing to listen
For exporting arms
For desiring dominance
For wanting to win
For lacking humility

For failing to risk
For failing to trust
For failing to act
For failing to negotiate
For failing to hope
For failing to love
For our arrogance
For our impatience
For our cowardice
For our pride
For our silence

That we learn compassion
...change our hearts
That we embrace nonviolence
That we act in justice
That we live in hope
That we might be strong
That we do your will
That we might be peace.

— *Pax Christi USA*

Little Litany of Praise

Creator God, we offer you our thanks.
For the gift of life, *we thank you, O God.*
For work and rest,...
For family and friends,...
For the warmth of the sun,...
For the cooling rain,...
For the moon and the stars,...
For the beauty of trees,...
For the loveliness of flowers,...
For the happiness of music,...
For the comforts of religion,...
For our special gifts and graces,...
For all our sorrows,...
For all your loving kindness,...

Almighty and eternal God,
grant that we may never forget to love you,
to adore you,
and to praise you in joy and in sorrow
all our lives long.

— *Blanche Jennings Thompson*

Litany to the Holy Name

Yours is the power and the glory
...let us love in your Holy Name
Yours is the radiance and light.
Yours is the love that brings all people together.
Yours is the love that breaks down all barriers
and divisions.
Yours is the love which casts out all fear.
Yours is the command that we act justly, love
tenderly and walk humbly with our God.
In love your yoke is easy and your burden light.

Litany of Women

Creator God, you who have given great women
throughout the ages, help us to draw strength
and courage from their lives.

Blessed be Eve, mother of the earth,
Blessed be her name.
Blessed be Sara, founder of the faith,
Blessed be her name.
Blessed be Rebecca, woman of courage,
Blessed be her name.
Blessed be Ruth, model of friendship,
Blessed be her name.
Blessed be Naomi, faithful woman,

Blessed be her name.
Blessed be Priscilla, early believer,
Blessed be her name.
Blessed be Joanna and Susanna, friends of
  Jesus,
Blessed be their name.
Blessed be Clare of Assisi, friend of the poor,
Blessed be her name.
Blessed be Hildegard of Bingen, artist and
  mystic,
Blessed be her name.
Blessed be Kateri Tekakwitha, first native
  American saint,
Blessed be her name.
Blessed be Theresa of Calcutta, protector of the
  dying,
Blessed be her name.
Blessed be Julian of Norwich, visionary,
Blessed be her name.
Blessed be Dorothy Day, patron of peacemakers,
Blessed be her name.
Blessed be Dorothy Kazel, Ita Ford, Maura
  Clark, and Jean Donovan, North American
  martyrs,
Blessed be their name.

Blessed be wives and mothers,
Blessed be their lives.
Blessed be daughters, sisters, and aunts,
Blessed be their lives.

Blessed be single women,
Blessed be their lives.
Blessed be women religious,
Blessed be their lives.
Blessed be old women,
Blessed be their lives.
Blessed be young women,
Blessed be their lives.
Blessed be poor women,
Blessed be their lives.

Blessed be all women:
    those who have gone before us,
    those present with us now,
    and those yet to come.

The Boat People Litany

Jesus, you calmed the waves...
    be with the boat people.
Jesus, you quieted the winds...
Jesus, you walked on the water...
Jesus, you slept in a boat...
Jesus, you chose boat people as apostles...
Jesus, you preached from a boat...
Until they find safe harbor...
Until their homeland is safe...
Until they are reunited
    with their families...

Until the hearts of the world
      are opened to their cries...

From our fear of strangers...
      Christ, deliver us.
From our fear of differences...
From our fear of the unknown...
From our fear of your message...
From our fear of your example...
From our deafness...
From our violence...
From our selfishness...
From our paralysis...
From our self-righteousness...

Toward the lonely...
      open our hearts.
Toward the hungry...
Toward the thirsty...
Toward the imprisoned...
Toward the exiled...
Toward the alien...
Toward the helpless...
Toward the voiceless...
Toward the poor...
Toward the homeless...
Toward all those whose needs we overlook...
Toward a more just sharing of what we have
      received...
Toward our sisters and brothers everywhere...

Be with those who suffer injustice... *Jesus, hear us*.

Be with those who oppose injustice... *Jesus, hear us*.

Be with those who flee injustice... *Jesus, we beg you, hear us*.

Let us pray,
Creator God, conscious of our oneness as your children, we beg you to open our hearts to all boat people. We pray in the Spirit who hovers over the sometimes chaotic waters of our world, calling us to share in the new creation announced by your son in whose name we pray, Jesus Christ. Amen.

— Jim Dinn

A Litany for African Americans

Creator God, you told us that without a vision the people will perish. We call on these visionaries, these dreamers who struggled against the sin of racism in our country.

We remember William Lloyd Garrison, founder of the New England Anti-slavery Society in 1832 ... *we will carry on the dream*

We remember Harriet Tubman, a former slave who helped lead escaped slaves to freedom.

We remember Rev. Eliah Lovejoy, a leading white abolitionist who was killed in 1837 while defending his printing press.

We remember Sojourner Truth, a fearless leader in the anti-slavery and women's rights movements.

We remember Frederick Douglass, a run-away slave who was a tireless worker for emancipation.

We remember Rosa Parks, a seamstress from Montgomery, Alabama who refused to sit in the back of the bus and the thousands who had the courage to join the Montgomery bus boycott.

We remember Medgar Evars, shot and killed while organizing voter registration in Mississippi, and all the others who lost their lives in the civil rights movement.

We remember Dorothy Counts, the first black student to attend Harding High School in Charlotte, NC and all other children who courageously broke down the walls of segregated schools.

We remember Martin Luther King, Jr., who
sounded the prophet's call to the entire nation,
and invited us to become the beloved community.

Loving God, give us the courage to stand against
the ignorance and blindness of racism. Give us
the grace to see through the false stereotypes
and fears that keep us apart. Open our hearts
and minds to your vision of the beloved community. Take us to the mountain top to see the
Promised Land, so that, in the midst of the
poverty and wealth, the despair and addiction,
the fear and hatred, we might be able to proclaim the good news of salvation. Amen.

— Pax Christi USA

Vows, Pledges and Creeds

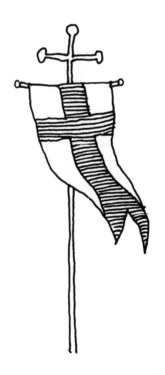

Just for Today

Today ... I will live in peace with my God, my neighbor and myself. I will bring peace to my patch of this earth.

Today ... I will believe that world peace is possible. I will remember that hope is the most important gift I can give my world.

Today ... I will not be a party to pessimism nor join the indifferent.

Today ... I will be happy. I will remember that my joy is up to me. I will carry my confidence to all I touch this day.

Today ... I will love my enemies. I will pray for them. I will try to see our differences from their point of view.

Today ... I will disarm myself of rage by extending my hand in help and forgiveness.

Today ... I will know that peace is the child of justice — that peace is more than the absence of war.

Today ... I will plant a seed of justice in this global village, in my city, in my neighborhood, in my family and in my heart.

Today ... I will pray for peace for all those with whom I come into contact.

Today ... I will test my love of peace by doing one act for peace.

Today ... I will stand with Christ the Peacemaker.

— Pax Christi USA

Vow of Nonviolence

Recognizing the violence in my own heart, yet trusting in the goodness and mercy of God, I vow for one year to practice the nonviolence of Jesus who taught us in the Sermon on the Mount:

> *Blessed are the peacemakers, for they shall be called the sons and daughters of God. ... You have learned how it was said, "You must love your neighbor and hate your enemy," but I say to you. "Love your enemies, and pray for those who persecute you. In this way, you will be daughters and sons of your Creator in heaven.*

Before God the Creator and the Sanctifying
Spirit, I vow to carry out in my life the love and
example of Jesus

- by striving for peace within myself and
  seeking to be a peacemaker in my daily
  life;
- by accepting suffering rather than
  inflicting it;
- by refusing to retaliate in the face of
  provocation and violence;
- by persevering in nonviolence of tongue
  and heart;
- by living conscientiously and simply so
  that I do not deprive others of
  the means to live;
- by actively resisting evil and working
  nonviolently to abolish war and the
  causes of war from my own heart and
  from the face of the earth.

God, I trust in Your sustaining love and believe
that just as You gave me the grace and desire to
offer this, so You will also bestow abundant
grace to fulfill it.

— *Pax Christi USA*

The Shakertown Pledge

Recognizing that the earth and the fullness thereof is a gift from our gracious God, and that we are called to cherish, nurture and provide loving stewardship for the earth's resources, and recognizing that life is a gift, and a call to responsibility, joy and celebration, I make the following declarations:

1. I declare myself to be a world citizen.

2. I commit myself to lead an ecologically sound life.

3. I commit myself to lead a life of creative simplicity and to share my personal wealth with the world's poor.

4. I commit myself to join with others in reshaping insititutions in order to bring about a more just global society in which each person has full access to the needed resources for their physical, emotional, intellectual and spiritual growth.

5. I commit myself to occupational accountability and in so doing I will seek to avoid the creation of products which cause harm to others.

6. I affirm the gift of my body, and commit myself to its proper nourishment and physical well-being.

7. I commit myself to examine continually my relations with others, and to attempt to relate honestly, morally, and lovingly to those around me.

8. I commit myself to personal renewal through prayer, meditation and study.

9. I commit myself to responsible participation in a community of faith.

A Pledge of Stewardship and Nonviolence

In the beginning, God, you created
the heavens, the earth and all living things
and said, "It is good."

We recognize the holiness of earth,
the oneness of humanity,
and the sacredness of all life.

Because we hold these beliefs in our hearts
we wish to model by our lives and actions
a commitment to steward this planet Earth
    as a blessing from God,
inherited from countless unknown ancestors.

We pledge to use these gifts of land, air and
water
    with gratitude,
    reverently,
    sparingly,
    justly,
preserving as much as possible
the natural beauties which surround us
so that succeeding generations
can receive them as our legacy.

Because we further believe
in the sacred value of every person,
we understand our duty to help create
a human community across the globe
which transcends national loyalties.

We therefore pledge ourselves
to open our hearts and homes to the guest,
especially the poor and the stranger,
to join with those who struggle for basic human
rights,
to respect those who hold opinions different from
our own,
to participate in dialogue to rid ourselves of
hatred,
to ask pardon of those we have offended,
seeking always to act in a spirit of nonviolence.

We make this pledge in the firm hope that our
actions will transform both ourselves and our

world into a society of justice and peace,
a foretaste of the reign of God promised to those
who love.

— Stephanie Campbell, OSB

World Citizen Pledge

I pledge allegiance to the flag of the united
states of the world, and to the community for
which it stands: one people loved into existence
by God, breathing an indivisible air, warmed by
the sun that shines on good and bad alike, kept
alive by rain that falls on the just and unjust.

I commit myself to spend my life for this
world, for liberty and justice for all. Amen.

— Mary Evelyn Jegen, SND

Creed for a Nuclear Age

We believe in Jesus Christ,
Crucified, risen and ascended,
Who has battled with evil and won.
He has won with the power of his love,
Love which is stronger than all the evil
        and violence in the world.
We believe in the power of his love,

Power alive in his people today,
Power to overcome fear and suspicion.
We put our trust in his love alone,
And we turn away from all nuclear weapons.
That kill our innocent brothers and sisters.
We cannot rely on the weapons of the world
When all our security, hope and life is in Jesus.

We believe in the power of the Risen Christ,
For only he can give us inward security.
We turn away from the evil of mass destruction,
Of arming ourselves while others starve,
Of trusting the weapons of evil
To safeguard the true and the good.
We believe in Jesus Christ;
And we trust his power of love and nothing else.

— *BCC Mannafest, Lincoln Cathedral, 1981.*

A Creed from Asia

We believe in the God of love, who calls us to
reject all idols and who seeks a deep communion
with us.

We believe in the God who is not remote
but who is immersed in the life of this world
sharing its hope and feeling its pain.

We believe in the God who identifies
with the poor and the oppressed and those who

long for faith and who calls us to stand with them.

We believe in the God whose love is vulnerable, whose heart is aching and whose covenant with all people is unshakeable.

— Christian Conference of Asia News

A Creed from South Africa

Jesus has taught us to speak of hope as the coming of God's Kingdom.

We believe that God is at work in our world turning hopeless and evil situations into good.

We believe that goodness and justice and love will triumph in the end, and that tyranny and oppression cannot last forever.

One day 'all tears will be wiped away' and 'the lamb will lie down with the lion.'

True peace and true reconciliation are not only desirable, they are assured and guaranteed.

This is our faith, and our hope.

*— Canadian Catholic Organization
for Development and Peace*

A Modern Creed

We are not alone, we live in God's world.
We believe in God:
who has created and is creating,
who has come in Jesus, the Word made flesh,
to reconcile and make new,
who works in us and others by the Spirit.

We trust in God.

We are called to be the Church:
to celebrate God's presence,
to love and serve others,
to seek justice and resist evil,
to proclaim Jesus, crucified and risen,
our judge and our hope.

In life, in death, in life beyond death,
God is with us.
We are not alone. Thanks be to God.

— United Church of Canada

Stations of
the Cross

This is an abridged version of *Stations of the Cross* by Megan McKenna, PhD.

The unabridged book may be obtained from Pax Christi USA.

STATIONS OF THE CROSS

First Station: Jesus Is Condemned to Death

We all stand under the sentence of death. But there is a death that is not part of the natural process of life, a death that is premeditated, unnecessary, violent, legal but unjust. Those in whom there is no guilt still die: children are abused, women are battered, the old are hidden away, the poor are deprived of human rights.

Jesus is the incarnation of the innocent condemned unjustly to death. The reign of God is found where these poor ones are welcomed and given life.

We stand as friends of the persecuted, committed to giving them life and giving more abundantly.

We adore you, Christ, and we bless you.
By the power of your holy cross help us
to change the world.

Second Station: Jesus Takes Up the Cross

Jesus, the poor one, bears the burden of his people. Carrying the cross, he carried them; he carries us. The cross is the whole history of hate, violence, rejection, and war. In accepting the cross, Jesus takes up the misery of humanity. The cross becomes God's complaint — there is no justice, mercy, or peace when the children of earth are despised, despoiled, and made to endure indignity.

We renew our baptismal promise to live under no other sign of power than the sign of the cross. We take up the burdens others carry and reject all that hinders us from following Jesus in the way of the cross.

We adore you, Christ, and we bless you.
By the power of your holy cross help us
to change the world.

Third Station: Jesus Falls the First Time

Jesus knew in his own body the force of violence, the power of fear and the domination of those intent on destroying him. All might, all evil, all hostility struck against him and he fell. But he stood again, faced the power of violence, and absorbed it within himself. Jesus' lifestyle of personal nonviolence was chosen long before he faced the cross and execution. His first word, "repent" was the call to be nonviolent and obedient.

Every time we fall, giving in to hatred and revenge, we promise to rise again and recommit ourselves to the nonviolent Jesus. We will strive to be peacemakers in our daily lives, offering an alternative to the violence that is so pervasive in our culture and world.

We adore you, Christ, and we bless you.
By the power of your holy cross help us to change the world.

Fourth Station: Jesus Meets His Mother

From the beginning Mary shared the fate of her child, including his call to prophecy, his rejection and sufferings. She prayed what he prayed — that the proud be overthrown in the conceit of their hearts, that the hungry be fed and the rich sent empty away, that the meek and lowly live with dignity and the powerful be dethroned. On the road to Calvary Mary stood with her son and endured humiliation, mocking and ridicule. She symbolizes all who stand in solidarity with those whose pain is public. She stands with women who have illegitimate children, with those who contact AIDS, with men and women marginalized because of their sexuality. And she stands with all who befriend them.

We commit ourselves to compassion, to openness and to accepting suffering in our lives rather than inflicting it. We pray for courage to support those rejected by society.

We adore you, Christ, and we bless you.
By the power of your holy cross help us
to change the world.

Fifth Station: Simon Helps Jesus Carry the Cross

With Simon we are pressed into service on behalf of others. We are recruited to help Jesus bestow our bread on the hungry, satisfy the afflicted, remove from our midst oppression, false accusations and malicious speech. These works of justice and mercy — actions we don't often choose for ourselves — teach us most about loving others unselfishly and accepting responsibility for them. We cannot pick and choose the people we love or help. Everyone is worthy of our care.

We recommit ourselves to act in solidarity with the poor, the victim, the outcast and to recruit others on their behalf.

Many Simons must respond to meet the pressing human needs in shelters, soup kitchens, houses of hospitality, hospices and places of sanctuary. Are we reluctant to associate with the poor, the victim, the outcast? Do we choose personal convenience over compassion, selfishness over self-sacrifice? Do we prefer to spend time, money and resources on personal wants while millions are without basic human needs? Do we seek the companionship of the comfortable rather than the friendship of the poor?

We recommit ourselves to act in solidarity
with the poor, the victim, the outcast and to
recruit others to work on their behalf.

We adore you, Christ, and we bless you.
By the power of your holy cross help us
to change the world.

Sixth Station: Veronica Wipes the Face of Jesus

Condemned prisoners have no rights, no
dignity, no humanity; they deserve no care, no
tenderness, no intimacy. Veronica knew that
aiding a condemned prisoner would incur the
wrath of the mob, yet she refused to yield to fear
and intolerance. In the face of derision and
rejection, she reached out in kindness, wiping
from Jesus' face the dirt and blood of hatred. For
her act of resistance she was given a glimpse of
the face of God.

We recommit ourselves to the practice of
charity, of being present to those rejected by
society. We promise to welcome them and to use
our own resources to touch and comfort them.

We adore you, Christ, and we bless you.
By the power of your holy cross help us
to change the world.

Seventh Station: Jesus Stumbles a Second Time

The violence of the system degrades, keeps down, rejects and never forgets failure and weakness. So many in our society fall again and again under the burden. We have names and categories for them: alcoholics, addicts, abusers. It's so easy to see them as problems rather than persons with individual stories. It's so easy to forget how many are victims of our failed educational, economic and legal systems, scapegoats of racism, sexism and intolerance. Actually, it's a miracle that the journey continues at all and that anyone marginalized by the system gets up again.

We remember that the power of God's Word is revealed in the work of our hands, in the call of the prophets and in the transformation of society. We commit ourselves to endure in this work.

We adore you, Christ, and we bless you.
By the power of your holy cross help us
to change the world.

Eighth Station: The Women of Jerusalem Weep for Jesus

For whom do we weep? Over whom do we weep? Our tears tell us whom we love? Shedding tears is a way of caring for others and being a part of them. Jesus wept over a city, a nation, a people who were lost, a people who refused his dream of peace.

Let us be still and weep in our own hearts. Let us weep for all those lost in our wars, in our armed conflicts, in our military maneuvers. Let us weep for all who suffer because our country initiates and aids racial and national conflicts with arms, money and supplies. May we recommit ourselves to penance, to mourning and to weeping for our part in the violence of despair.

We adore you, Christ, and we bless you.
By the power of your holy cross help us
to change the world.

Ninth Station: Jesus Falls the Third Time

As Jesus neared the end of the way, he was tired, afraid and had little strength left. It is when we are vulnerable that we are most likely to fall. How difficult it is to struggle to our feet and begin again.

The world knows this and tries to destroy men and women who stand against injustice. Torture, illegal imprisonment, malicious lies are designed to beat the bodies and whip the spirits of those who proclaim freedom and hope to the people.

After falling a third time, Jesus refused to surrender and rose to face his fate and confront his executioners — a person in possession of self and of truth. Sustain us, Jesus, with your steadfast spirit.

We adore you, Christ, and we bless you.
By the power of your holy cross help us
to change the world.

Tenth Station: Jesus Is Stripped of His Garments

The violence of the arms race and nuclear war madly flings the earth toward destruction. The threat of death hovering over nations is the harshest indignity for human beings to bear. Why? Because all humanity is one and our glory is that of the children of God.

In baptism our bodies become temples, dwelling places for God. No longer slaves to violence, our bodies are now instruments of justice and reconciliation. With our bodies we promise to make peace by nonviolently resisting evil. With our bodies we promise to create a sacred space that brings life to a weary, war-torn world.

God, we stand before you, naked in body and spirit. You alone know the violence raging within us. Give us the grace to disarm our hearts. May we be stripped of everything that provokes violence, causes division and demeans humanity.

We adore you, Christ, and we bless you.
By the power of your holy cross help us
to change the world.

Eleventh Station: Jesus Is Nailed to the Cross

Jesus is executed by being nailed to a piece of wood, hung naked, exposed to taunts, reduced to an object of ridicule. Public crucifixions continue today, only in place of wooden beams there is a gas chamber, electric chair, injection, firing squad. The death penalty is not our right.

O God, forgive us for we know not what we do. Help us to work against the death penalty, to stand against legally sanctioned death.

We adore you, Christ, and we bless you.
By the power of your holy cross help us
to change the world.

Twelfth Station: Jesus Dies on the Cross

It is done. It is finished.

But what is over. Certainly not the life of Jesus, not his promise of the victory of justice and peace and freedom? No, the reign of God is just beginning.

What is done and finished is the reign of destruction, violence, death and sin. Now the peace of God reigns, but what a harsh and dreadful peace it is. Do you want to be a peacemaker? Jesus shows us that in being stretched between two enemies we become reconcilers, transforming enmity into love, adversaries into friends. Peace comes through nonviolently resisting injustice unto death.

O God, into your hands we commend our lives. Incarnate in us the peace of Christ and give us to the world.

We adore you, Christ, and we bless you.
By the power of your holy cross help us
to change the world.

Thirteenth Station: Jesus Is Taken Down from the Cross

What did Jesus have to show for his life when it ended?

Many of his friends abandoned him for fear of being killed. Some watched from a distance. Only a few companions remained to bury him, quickly, before the sun went down.

All that Jesus took to the grave was the certainty that he had done the will of God. He came among us to give life and give it more abundantly and he fulfilled that mission.

We all have the same reason for living. How will we know if our lives have been worthwhile? The criteria is clear. Will others remember us for our mercy, our kindness, our truth-telling, our compassion, our faithfulness. Have we, in other words, done the will of God?

Help us to remember, Jesus, that in the evening of life we will be judged by our love.

We adore you, Christ, and we bless you.
By the power of your holy cross help us
to change the world.

Fourteenth Station: Jesus Is Laid in the Tomb

The body of Jesus was returned to the earth. It was interred with the waste, the refuse of society. The earth took back its creator and maker. The womb of Mother the Earth received the flesh of the Sun of Justice, just as Father the Sky embraced his last cry and prayer. All of earth groans and is in agony, awaiting resurrection. A few followers, too, wait in hope, ready to witness to what is still invisible, the glorious freedom of the children of God, the coming to fullness of justice and peace.

O God, be merciful to us your children. Let us be signs of hope and peace in the world and give you glory by our lives.

We adore you, Christ, and we bless you.
By the power of your holy cross help us
to change the world.

Fifteenth Station: The Resurrection

"Peace be with you"...and he showed them his hands and his side. By pointing to his wounds, Jesus reminds us of the price of peace. Peace is the gift of death endured, of the struggle for justice sought after, of forgiveness rendered to friend and enemy alike. Peace is the gift of resistance continued, of the cross embraced, of the poor welcomed into our lives. Peace is a gift given to us today. In the body of the crucified, in the sufferings of the poor, and in the way of the cross is our peace.

This is our faith. This is the faith of the believing community. Let us go now to await our resurrection and the Risen One's presence among us again. Let us await the coming of justice, of peace in our midst. Peace be with you.

We adore you, Christ, and we bless you.
By the power of your holy cross help us
to change the world.

Fasting

Fasting

In their pastoral, *The Challenge of Peace*, the US Catholic bishops call the Christian community to fast for the cause of peace.

As a tangible sign of our need and desire to do penance, we, for the cause of peace, commit ourselves to fast and abstinence on each Friday of the year. We call upon our people voluntarily to do penance on Friday by eating less food and by abstaining from meat. This return to a traditional practice of penance, once well observed in the US church, should be accompanied by works of charity and service toward our neighbors. Each Friday should be a day significantly devoted to prayer, penance and almsgiving for peace.

— *The Challenge of Peace, par. 298*

A Reflection on Fasting

The New Testament's answer to the question, "Why should we fast?" is "As a sign of your love." Fasting is not an end in itself. Love has to do with relationships, and fasting can lead us to a better understanding of our essential relationships with ourselves, with others, with the planet earth, and with God. Fasting and abstinence may well be a starting point for spiritual growth toward greater love among the well-fed congregations in this affluent society, protected by a bloated nuclear arsenal.

The New Testament does not guarantee a positive outcome for fasting. Fasting may make people self-righteous, doctrinaire, even contemptuous. Fasting can get side-tracked into dieting. Fasting which will result in deepening love must begin in love and abide in it. Yet a loving decision to forego the joy of uncontrolled eating for a single day out of each seven can put us in touch immediately with our dependence on our own gratification for a sense of well-being. Our initial efforts to fast may reveal that we do indeed live "by bread alone." What then?

A time of fasting is a time of testing human readiness to wait on God. Do we trust that God lives, that God cares, that God loves and keeps the earth and all who live on it? Have we the humility to yield control to God? Fasting in faith can lead us more deeply into into the mystery of God with us and in us, and so restore human hope grown weary, love grown cold.

The New Testament regularly associates fasting and prayer and almsgiving. So does the peace pastoral. Both prayer and almsgiving move the center of our fasting beyond our preoccupation with ourselves toward a center of love. If we dare to discover hunger symbolically through a day of fasting each week, a further decision to complement that fast with almsgiving will force us to look around for hungry people.

A day of fasting and involvement with the hungry can draw us further into understanding the complexity of our social reality. We might become more curious about the fat defense budgets and their relationship to unemployment, underemployment, inflation, empty stomachs. We might get more interested in the chain of world food production , which keeps our super-markets and tables loaded while keeping the world's agricultural workers malnourished, feeding instead the workers' resentment of us and our way of life.

This simple discipline, practiced and continu-ally reflected on, can be a sign of our deepening conversion to the mystery of a love powerful enough to redeem the world.

— *Mary Collins, OSB*

Prayer for Fasting

All praise be yours, God our Creator,
as we wait in joyful hope
for the flowering of justice
and the fullness of peace.

All praise for this day.
By our weekly fasting and prayer,
cast out the spirit of war, of fear and mistrust,
and make us grow hungry
    for human kindness,
thirsty for solidarity
    with all the people of your dear earth.

May all our prayer, our fasting and our deeds
be done in the name of Jesus. Amen.

> — *Archdiocese of Chicago*
> *Office for the Ministry of Peace*
> *and Justice*

Readings on Fasting

Every. . . religion of any importance appreciates
the spiritual value of fasting. . . . For one thing,
identification with the starving poor is a mean-
ingless term without the experience behind it.
But I quite agree that even a eighty-day fast may
fail to rid a person of pride, selfishness, ambition
and the like. Fasting is merely a prop. But as a
prop to a tottering structure is of essential value,
so is the prop of fasting of inestimable value for a
struggling soul. **Gandhi**

As for me, I did not suffer at all from the hunger
or headache or nausea which usually accompa-
nies the first few days of a fast, but I had offered
my fast in part for the victims of famine all over
the world, and it seemed to me that I had very
special pains. They were certainly of a kind I
have never had before, and they seemed to me to
pierce to the very marrow of my bones when I lay
down at night. **Dorothy Day (after a 10-day
fast during the second Vatican Council
urging the bishops to issue a strong peace
statement)**

Fasting has always been an important part of
our farm worker movement. We learned from
Gandhi and other spiritual leaders before him
the value of fasting for such personal purposes as
preparation for a significant life event, atone-

ment, and self-purification. . . . We also learned from Gandhi that the value of fasting could be extended beyond the personal to the social: that a person who fasted and suffered for a much-needed societal change broader than his or her purposes could elicit from others the desire to share the suffering and thereby participate in eradicating a specific social injustice. **Cesar Chavez**

My urgency increases, Nguyen Thi Yen. I will fast from all solid food until you are free and reunited with your mother, until you can climb the coconut trees and pluck papaya from sunny branches. If I cannot know the brokenness, the blood your body has lost, let me at least learn simplicity and directness to work for your life. . . . I hope some of its spirit, those parts which emerge effortlessly, will reach you like the almost-sound of a bird's wings. **Mobi Warren (At 19, she fasted in solidarity with Nguyen Thi Yen, a student who was arrested and tortured during the Vietnam War.)**

Examination
of Conscience

Examination of Conscience

An examination of conscience is a way to hold ourselves accountable before God and each other for the evil we do and the good we do not do. Some refer to it as an examination of consciousness: scanning our motives, thoughts, and actions to detect our loyalty to or betrayal of the priorities of the reign of God.

The delicate and difficult part in this process involves what we hold as our guide for accountability. For centuries the blueprint for good conduct was the list of Ten Commandments, until Jesus proposed a very different set of guidelines with the beatitudes (Matthew 5:1-13).

As early as A.D. 150 in a document written by the Shepherd of Hermas, the beatitudes were accepted as the positive norm of morality for Christians, stressing the ideals of their founder and avoiding the "do nots" of the decalogue.

What follows is an examination of conscience and consciousness based on the beatitudes. It makes sense only if we truly believe that the teachings of Jesus have practical applicability in the world in which each of us lives and breathes. If we admit that relevance, we will find enough power in our fidelity to these counsels to renew the face of the earth.

1. "Blessed are the poor in spirit, for theirs is the kingdom of heaven."
   - Do I fear being poor, in spirit or otherwise, and prefer to be rich in money, brains, or influence?
   - Is my desire for poverty of spirit congruent with my lifestyle?
   - Do I use the word of God to rationalize my lifestyle, or am I willing to have God's word criticize it?
   - Do I cling to my own ideas, opinions and judgments, sometimes to the point of idolatry?
   - Do I contribute my time, talent and money to the poor of the world?
   - Do I make it my business to examine the causes of poverty in our world and work to eradicate unjust systems?

2. "Blessed are those who mourn, for they shall be comforted."
   - Do I grieve over loneliness, despair, guilt and rejection in the lives of others?
   - Am I willing to admit my own despondencies and need for comfort?
   - Do I minister consolation and healing, or do I blandly encourage people to "have courage," thereby avoiding the opportunity to mourn with another?

- Am I doing anything to dry the tears of those who mourn over war, poverty, hunger, injustice?

3. "Blessed are the meek, for they shall inherit the earth."
   - Do I see any value in meekness or nonviolence?
   - Do I cringe at the thought of being called meek?
   - Do I understand nonviolence as a way to fight evil with good, and do I choose to live that way?
   - How much are intimidation and force part of my lifestyle?
   - Do I work for nonviolent social change?
   - Do I foster a cooperative spirit in my children?

4. "Blessed are those who hunger and thirst for righteousness, for they shall be satisfied.
   - Have I kept myself ignorant of important current events that are manifestations of injustice?
   - Are my energies and passions focused on Christ, or are they scattered, disordered, divided?
   - Am I honestly trying to improve the quality of life around me? Am I trying to improve the environment, racial relations,

care for the unborn, sexual equality, the lives of the poor and destitute?
- Have I decided that I will not be satisfied until justice is fulfilled in my own life, within my family, my church, my community, my world?
- Have I let fear keep me silent when I should have spoken out against prejudice, injustice and violence?

5. "Blessed are the merciful, for they shall obtain mercy."
- Do I operate on a double standard of expecting mercy but not wanting to grant it?
- Do I prefer the strict law and order approach, or that of mercy, tenderness and compassion?
- Are there places in my life where people are suffering because of me and my unforgiving attitude?
- Am I devoid of a merciful spirit towards those I call "enemy"?
- What is my attitude toward capital punishment, ex-convicts...?

6. "Blessed are the pure in heart, for they shall see God."
- Am I trusting and trustful?
- Do I value living without pretense, or am I constantly fearful that someone will take

advantage of me?
- Am I open and honest about who I am and what I do?
- Do I deflect the attention and honor due to God and claim these things for myself?
- Have I been untrue to myself, even a little, for advancement, money or good opinion?
- Have I failed to take time for prayer, solitude, reflection?

7. "Blessed are the peacemakers for they shall be called children of God."
- Am I eager for reconciliation, or do I antagonize and yearn for revenge?
- Do I think apologizing is a sign of weakness?
- Am I willing to be a bridge in family and community arguments?
- Do I support violence in films, television and sports?
- Have I studied peace and taken initiatives to stop violence and war?
- Have I read, and do I support, the many official church statements against the arms race, nuclear weapons, war?
- Do I see the Christian vocation as one of peacemaker?
- Is my presence a source of peace to those around me?

8. "Blessed are those who are persecuted for righteousness' sake, for theirs is the kingdom of heaven. Blessed are you when people revile you and persecute you and utter all kinds of evil against you falsely on my account."

- Do I criticize or ridicule those who suffer for their beliefs?
- Am I embarrassed to step out of the mainstream to stand up for a principle?
- Who are my heroes? Are there any among them who gave their lives without vengeance for what is true?
- Would I do the same?
- Do I worship security and fear costly discipleship?
- Have I called myself Christian without making my life a witness to the teachings of Jesus?
- Have I openly supported those who defend justice and give their lives for peace?

9. "Rejoice and be glad, for your reward is great in heaven."

- Do I live confident of the promises of Jesus?
- Do I surrender to pessimism and anxiety?
- Do I perceive that there is a paradoxical victory in the cross of Jesus that breaks through power structures and conquers in peace and love?

• Have I become cynical rather than hopeful?

— *Doris Donnelly*

Reflections on Becoming
an Instrument of Peace

"Where there is hatred let me sow love" challenges me to take seriously the radical absurdity of the Gospel precept"Love your enemies." So we wonder ... suppose I were to commit myself to spend fifteen minutes once a week, with the St. Francis Prayer as the focus, with the aim of becoming more available as an instrument of peace? How might I use that time?

On different occasions I might use one of the following approaches?

1.   St. Francis used the greeting "God give you Peace." Does God give me peace in my heart? Is there some part of my life which most needs reconciliation and forgiveness by being acknowledged in my prayer? If so, what first step can I take today?

2.   Is there a personal relationship in my life
that stands unreconciled? Does it wait for my
willingness —
a) to be forgiven by God
b) to forgive myself
c) to be forgiven by someone else
d) to forgive someone else
e) to be the one to take the first step ... and if so,
what first step can I take today:

3.   Is there a relationship or situation close to
me which is unreconciled for lack of a peacemaker? Does it wait for me to take the risk of
getting caught in the middle? And if so, what
first step can I take today?

4.   Are there any people of peace whose courageous stand on a vital issue I admire? Am I
praying for them? Have I let them know they
have my support? By a letter? A phone-call? A
gift? And if not, what first step can I take today?

5.   Are there any who claim to be people of
peace with whose stand on vital issues I strongly
disagree? Am I praying for them? Have I let
them know, in truth and love, my own concern in
this issue? And if not, what first step can I take
today?

6.   Are there whole categories of people by
nation, color, class, political stance, etc., towards

whom I feel fear (out of ignorance?), anger, resentment, or indignation? Am I praying for them, and myself? And if not, what first step can I take today?

7.   Do I call the attention of my political representatives to important issues of peace and justice? Am I praying for them? How can I express my concerns? How can I become involved? What first step can I take today?

— The Franciscan

Symptoms of Inner Peace

— an unmistakable ability to enjoy each moment.
— loss of interest in judging others.
— loss of interest in interpreting actions of others.
— loss of interest in conflict.
— loss of ability to worry.
— frequent, overwhelming episodes of appreciation.
— contented feelings of connectedness with others and nature.
— frequent attacks of smiling through the eyes from the heart.

— tendency to let things happen rather than make them happen.
— tendency to think and act spontaneously rather than from fear based on past experiences.
— susceptibility to love extended by others as well as the uncontrollable urge to extend love.

— author unknown

Meditative
Prayer

by Mary Lou Kownacki, OSB

Meditation

"Be still and know that I am God" the psalmist urges us. Perhaps that's another way of
saying that God is always present to us and our
task is to become more aware of that presence.

Meditative prayer, reflective prayer in
silence and solitude, is one way to "know God" in
a deeper way. The idea behind meditative prayer
is a simple but potent one: if we devote time each
day to reflective prayer, we can change. The
change will probably not be dramatic, just a
daily smoothing of the sharp edges of selfishness,
fear, falsehood. But if we are truly present to
God and do not harden our hearts, a new person
can emerge. A person empty of selfishness, of
fear, of ego; a person who looks at life and
humanity through divine eyes; a person whose
heartbeat is one with God's.

The following are some suggested methods
for meditative prayer.

Lectio Divina

Lectio divina (sacred reading) is a simple
method of praying the Scripture. To begin, call to
mind the abiding presence of God by reciting a
short prayer, or listening to a hymn, lighting a
candle. . . . Then pick up the Scripture or any
spiritual classic and slowly read or listen to the
Word. When you come to a sentence, phrase, or
word that attracts you, stop and repeat the text,

savoring its goodness and sweetness. After receiving the Word, it is time to respond by actively reflecting on the text and asking God to help you apply it to your life. What does God want you to hear today as you dwell upon this text? You may converse with God mentally or write down your insights and conversation in a scripture journal. After about fifteen or twenty minutes you may close lectio with a short prayer, bow, blowing out the candle . . . (Recommended book: *Too Deep For Words* - Thelma Hall)

Jesus Prayer

The Jesus Prayer, one of the most ancient and simple forms of meditative prayer, is given to us from the Greek and Russian Orthodox tradition. It consists of constantly repeating the prayer, "Lord Jesus Christ, Son of the Living God, have mercy on me" or just the holy name, "Jesus" or "Jesus, mercy."

A way to practice the Jesus Prayer is to repeat it often during the day and/or to set aside a definite time each day for the prayer. To begin the time period, try to quiet yourself and call upon God to be with you. Then slowly and reflectively repeat the Jesus Prayer over and over. Try to think of the words themselves and not any images or ideas. By constantly repeating the Holy Name, it is possible that we can be transformed into the prayer itself. People will see in us the compassion, the nonviolence, the

love of Jesus. (Recommended book: *The Way of
the Pilgrim*)

Mindfulness

The Buddhist monk Thich Nhat Hanh
speaks of mindfulness — keeping one's consciousness alive to the present moment — as a
way to practice meditation during the day. For
example:

Washing the dishes

Wash the dishes relaxingly as though each
bowl is an object of contemplation. Consider each
bowl as sacred. Follow your breath to prevent
your mind from straying. Do not try to hurry to
get the job over with. Consider washing the
dishes as the most important thing in life.
Washing the dishes is meditation. If you cannot
wash the dishes in mindfulness, neither can you
meditate while sitting in silence.

Compassion for an enemy

Sit quietly. Breathe and smile a half-smile.
Contemplate the image of the person who has
caused you suffering. Regard the features you
hate or despise the most or find the most repul-
sive. Try to examine what makes this person
happy and what causes suffering in his or her
daily life. Contemplate the person's perceptions:
try to see what patterns of thought and reason
this person follows. Examine what motivates this

person's hopes and actions. Finally consider the person's consciousness. See whether the person's views and insights are open and free or not, and whether he or she has been influenced by any prejudices, narrow-mindedness, hatred or anger. Continue until you feel compassion rise in your heart like a well filling with fresh water and your anger and resentment disappear. Practice this exercise many times on the same person.

(Recommended book: *The Miracle of Mindfulness* — Thich Nhat Hanh)

Any form of these suggested prayer forms and countless others (listening to music, gazing at an icon, chanting, reflective walking, liturgical dance) can help us become more aware of the God in whose presence we live and move and have our being.

Centering Prayer

A popular form of meditative prayer today is centering prayer. To practice centering prayer, choose a sacred word that expresses your love and desire for God. Some prayer words might be God, Jesus, Spirit, Love, Maranatha. . . . Then sit quietly and comfortably with eyes closed and silently repeat the word you have chosen for about 20 minutes. When you become aware of thought, return gently to the sacred word. At the end of the prayer period slowly recite a memorized prayer; e.g., the Prayer of Jesus. Again, the practice of centering prayer can transform us from within and lead to greater union with God. (Recommended Book: *Open Mind, Open Heart* — Thomas Keating)

Repetition of Sacred Passage

Another way of meditating is to slowly repeat prayers or passages from sacred scriptures. Again, the idea is to quiet yourself, close your eyes, call upon the Spirit and slowly recite the memorized prayer or scripture, concentrating on the words and the One to whom you pray. There are many prayers in this book that are excellent for meditation, including the psalms, the peace prayers, etc. (Recommended book: *Meditation* — Eknath Easwaran)

Readings for
the Journey

It is when things go wrong, when things good things do not happen, when our prayers seem to have been lost, that God is most present. We do not need the sheltering wings when things go smoothly. We are closest to God in the darkness, stumbling along blindly.

— *Madeleine L'Engle*

Pray as you can and do not try to pray as you can't. Take yourself as you find yourself; start from that.

— *Dom Chapman*

When you arise in the morning, give thanks for the morning light, for your life and strength. Give thanks for your food and for the joy of living. If you see no reason for giving thanks, the fault lies in yourself.

— *Indian proverb*

Thich Nhat Hanh: "I spoke at a Buddhist meeting; I said, 'In order to save the world, each of us has to build a pagoda.' "

Dan Berrigan: "To build a pagoda?"

Nhat Hanh: "Yes. To build a pagoda. There were people who thought that I was urging them to build more pagodas so Buddhism would become a national religion. But this pagoda cannot be built by stones and sticks and things like that, because this pagoda is a sanctuary where you have a chance to be alone and face yourself, the reality of yourself. If you don't have a pagoda like that to go to each day, several times a day, then you cannot protect the Eucharist, you cannot protect yourself, and you cannot protect the world from destruction."

— *The Raft is Not the Shore*

The Zen people say that you should sit in meditation as if a samurai was standing in front of you with sword upheld, ready to kill you with a single stroke. In this way you constantly face death. And the time comes when, liberated from the fear of death, you are filled with enlightenment and joy.

— *William Johnston*

Prayer is our humble answer to the inconceivable surprise of living. It is all we can offer in return for the mystery by which we live. . . . Amidst the meditation of mountains, the humility of flowers — wiser than all alphabets — clouds that die constantly for the sake of God's glory, we are hating, hunting, hurting. Suddenly we feel ashamed of our clashes and complaints in face of the tacit glory in nature. It is so embarrassing to live! How strange we are in the world, and how presumptuous our doings! Only one response can maintain us: gratefulness for witnessing the wonder, for the gift of our unearned right to serve, to adore, and to fulfill. It is gratefulness which makes the soul great.

— *Rabbi Abraham Heschel*

When you are in love with someone, it seems that the face of the beloved is before you when you drive, when you type, when you are taking out insurance, and so on. Somehow or other we can encompass these two realities, the face of the beloved and whatever we happen to be doing. Prayer is like that.

— *Catherine deHueck Doherty*

How can you define prayer, except by saying that it is love? It is love expressed in speech, and love expressed in silence. To put it another way, prayer is the meeting of two loves: the love of God and our love.

— *Catherine deHueck Doherty*

Forever at God's door
I gave my heart and soul. My fortune too.
I've no flock any more,
no other work in view.
My occupation: love. It's all I do.

— *St. John of the Cross*

Your prayer will take countless forms because it is the echo of your life, and a reflection of the inexhaustible light in which God dwells.

— *"Rule for a New Brother"*

Into this world,
this demented inn,
in which there is no room
for him at all,
Christ has come uninvited.
But because he cannot
be at home in it,
because he is
out of place in it, . . .
His place is with those
who do not belong,
who are rejected
by power because
they are regarded as weak,
those who are discredited,
who are denied
the status of persons,
tortured and exterminated.
With those for whom
there is no room,
Christ is present in this world.
He is mysteriously present
in those for whom
there seems to be nothing
but the world at its worst.

— *Thomas Merton*

All real prayer must begin in wonder.

— Ted Dunne, SJ

To pray is to descend with the mind into the heart, and there to stand before the face of God — ever present, all-seeing, within you.

— Theophane the Recluse

A lot of trouble about prayer would disappear if we only realized — really realized, and not just supposed that it was so — that we go to pray not because we love prayer but because we love God.

— Hubert van Zeller, OSB

Do what you can and then pray that God will give you the power to do what you cannot.

— St. Augustine

In the twilight of life, God will not judge us on our earthly possessions and human success, but rather on how much we have loved.

— St. John of the Cross

A disciple has been calling on God for many
years through prayer, fasting and meditation.
one day she hears a voice within her ask:
"Who is there?"
"At last, at last," she thinks joyfully.
"God." she cries. "It is me. It is me."
But she is met by silence and the voice disap-
pears.
Years pass and the woman goes on meditating
and calling on God with renewed passion.
Suddenly, without warning,
she hears the voice again.
"Who is there?"
This time, without hesitation, she replies,
"Only thou, only thou."
And the door opens and she enters the heart of
God.

— *source unknown*

All creation teaches us some way of prayer.

— *Thomas Merton*

By a long process of prayerful discipline I have
ceased for over forty years to hate anybody.

— *Gandhi*

An old Hindu saint settled under two trees
in a country infested by robbers.
He called his hut The Home of Peace.
One night a robber broke into the hut
in search of money.
With his dagger drawn, the thief crept toward
the monk.
The monk was sitting very still,
wrapped in deep prayer.
Just as the robber got ready to plunge the knife,
the old monk opened his eyes.
There was absolutely no fear in them.
Instead, he looked at the robber
with great compassion and tenderness.
The robber hesitated.
then dropped his dagger and fell to his knees.
The old monk rose and put his arms
around the would-be murderer.

Thought: The ways to realize God are not many,
but only one — love.

— source unknown

He goes to the edge of the cliff and turns his face
to the rising sun, and scatters the sacred corn-
meal. Then he prays for all the people. He asks
that we may have rain and corn and melons, and
that our fields may bring us plenty. But these
are not the only things he prays for. He prays

that all the people may have health and long life
and be happy and good in their hearts. And
Hopis are not the only people he prays for. He
prays for everybody in the whole world —
everybody. And not people alone; Lololomai
prays for all the plants. He prays for everything
that has life. That is how Lololomai prays.

— *Lololomai*

The guarantee of one's prayer is not in saying a
lot of words.
The guarantee of one's petition is very easy to
know:
    How do I treat the poor?
        — because that is where God is.
The degree to which you approach them,
or the scorn with which you approach them —
    that is how you approach your God.
What you do to them, you do to God.
The way you look at them is the way you look at
God.

—*Archbishop Oscar Romero*

Prayer is necessary. Without it we see only our point of view, our own righteousness, and ignore the perspective of our enemies. Prayer breaks down those distinctions. To do violence to others, you must make them enemies. Prayer, on the other hand, makes enemies into friends. When we have brought our enemies into our hearts in prayer, it becomes most difficult to maintain the hostility necessary for violence. In bringing them close to us, prayer serves to protect our enemies. Thus prayer undermines the propaganda and policies of governments designed to make us hate and fear our enemies. By softening our hearts toward our adversaries, prayer can become treasonous. Fervent prayer for our enemies is a great obstacle to war and the feelings that lead to it.

— *Jim Wallis*

Prayer and sacrifice must be used as the most
effective spiritual weapons in the war against
war, and like all weapons, they must be used
with deliberate aim: not just with a vague
aspiration for peace and security, but against
violence and war. This implies that we are also
willing to sacrifice and restrain our own instinct
for violence and aggressiveness in our relations
with other people. We may never succeed in this
campaign, but whether we succeed or not, the
duty is evident.

— *Thomas Merton*

Thou movest us to delight in praising Thee, for
Thou hast formed us for Thyself, and our hearts
are restless till they find rest in Thee.

— *St. Augustine of Hippo*

It's a barren prayer that does not go hand in
hand with alms.

— *St. Cyprian*

There were three friends who were eager workers, and one of them chose to devote himself to
making peace between people who were fighting,
in accordance with "Blessed are the peacemakers."

The second chose to visit the sick.

The third when off to live in tranquility in
the desert.

The first toiled away at the quarrels of men
and women, but could not resolve them all, and
so, went to the one who was looking after the
sick, and he found him flagging too, not succeeding in fulfilling the commandment. So the two of
them agreed to go and visit the one who was
living in the desert. They told him of their
difficulty and asked him to tell them what he
had been able to do. He was silent for a time,
then he poured water in a bowl and said to them,
"Look at the water." It was all turbulent. A little
later he told them to look at it again, and see
how the water had settled down. When they
looked at it, they saw their own faces as in a
mirror. Then he said to them, "In the same way
when you live in the midst of others you do not

see your own sins because of all the disturbance,
but if you become tranquil, especially in the
desert, then you can see your own shortcomings.

— *Desert Fathers and Mothers*

My greatest weapon is mute prayer.

— *Gandhi*

And then there is the question of prayer, which
consists for the most part in insisting that God
do for us what we are unwilling to do for one
another. Resolve: Let's do for one another what
we would have God do for all. This is known as
God-like activity.

— *Daniel Berrigan, SJ*

Helder Camara rises each morning at 2 a.m. to
pray. Dorothy Day has probably written as much
on prayer in her column in the Catholic Worker
as on any other subject. Yet despite the example
and unequivocal exhortations of the best of the
best, the Catholic peace movement does not seem
to possess a prayer life consistent with the
gravity of the evil it is confronting. It is almost
as if it were trying to carry on its war against the
powers of darkness with one of its most potent
weapons in mothballs.

— *Charles McCarthy*

On praying with open, outstretched hands: On
one occasion I gained new insight into this
ancient gesture, when I read somewhere that the
Assyrians had a word for prayer which meant "to
open the fist." The fist, and especially a fist
raised threateningly, is the sign of a highhanded,
even violent person. People grasp things in
closed hands when they are unwilling to let go of
them; they use clenched fists to assault and hurt
and, even worse, to beat others down so that
they cannot get up.

Those who pray, however, are saying
before God that they are renouncing all high-
handedness, all pride in their own sufficiency, all
violence. They open their fists. They hold up
their empty hands to God: "I have nothing that I

have not received from you, nothing that you have not placed in my empty hands. Therefore I do not keep a frantic hold on anything you have given me; therefore, too, I desire not to strike and hurt but only to give and to spread happiness and joy. For I myself am dependent on the One who fills my empty hands with gifts."

— *Balthasar Fischer*

Pure love and prayer are learned in the hour when prayer has become impossible and your heart has turned to stone.

— *Thomas Merton*

We cannot begin to grow in nonviolence except through prayer, fasting and solitude. Every program of nonviolence, whether of Gandhi, Martin Luther King or St. Francis of Assisi, has emphasized that the beginning of nonviolence is prayer, fasting and the gift of self. Then out of that come expressions of nonviolence. Nonviolence is not a tactic or series of actions, it is a form of prayer that becomes a realization of the kingdom.

— *James W. Douglass*

Prayer is the basis of all peacemaking precisely because in prayer we come to the realization that we do not belong to the world in which conflicts and wars take place, but to Jesus who offers us his peace. The paradox of peacemaking is indeed that we can only speak of peace in this world when our sense of who we are is not anchored in the world. We can only say, "We are for peace," when those who are fighting have no power over us.

— Henri Nouwen

One day a boy was watching a holy man praying on the banks of a river in India. When the holy man completed his prayer, the boy went over and asked him, "Will you teach me to pray?"

The holy man studied the boy's face carefully. Then he gripped the boy's head in his hands and plunged it forcefully into the water. The boy struggled frantically, trying to free himself in order to breathe. Finally, the holy man released his hold.

When the boy was able to get his breath, he gasped, "What did you do that for?" The holy man said, "I just gave you the first lesson."

"What do you mean?" asked the astonished boy.

"Well," said the holy man, "when you long to pray as much as you longed to breathe when your head was under water — only then will I be able to teach you to pray."

— *source unknown*

We have to remember that work is not prayer. It is at best an extension of prayer. We fool ourselves if we argue that we don't have to pray because we work so hard or our work is so good. Those who work without prayer — no matter how good the work, no matter how sincere the minister — soon dry up inside. They have nothing left to give. Or, the work fails and they have no faith to sustain them, no perspective to encourage them. More important, real prayer makes us more effective people because real prayer changes us. Prayer delivers us from our own internal oppressions, the burdens we put on ourselves, the bitterness we carry, because it enables the inbreaking of God in our lives.

— *Joan Chittister, OSB*

If the only prayer you say in your life is "thank you," that would suffice.

— *Meister Eckhart*

At the heart of silence is prayer. At the heart of
prayer is faith. At the heart of faith is life. At the
heart of life is service.

— *Mother Teresa*

A rabbi entered a room in his home, saw his son
deep in prayer. In the corner stood a cradle with
a crying baby. The rabbi asked his son, "Can't
you hear? There's a baby crying in this room."
The son said, "Father, I was lost in God." And
the rabbi said, "One who is lost in God can see
the very fly crawling up the wall."

— *Abel Herzberg*

Real prayer penetrates to the marrow of our soul
and leaves nothing untouched. The prayer of the
heart is prayer that does not allow us to limit our
relationship with God to interesting words or
pious emotion. . . . In our hearts we come to see
ourselves as sinners embraced by the mercy of
God. Thus the prayer of the heart is the prayer
of truth.

— *Henri Nouwen*

Prayer is not just spending time with God. It is
partly that — but if it ends there, it is fruitless.
No, prayer is dynamic. Authentic prayer changes
us — unmasks us — strips us — indicates where
growth is needed. Authentic prayer never leads
to complacency, but needles us — makes us
uneasy at times. It leads us to true self-knowl-
edge, to true humility.

— Teresa of Avila

Seek peace in your own place. You cannot find
peace anywhere save in your own self. In the
psalm we read: "There is no peace in my bones
because of my sin." When you make peace within
yourself, you will be able to make peace in the
whole world.

— Rabbi Bunam

If others speak ill of you,
praise them always.
If others injure you,
serve them nicely.
If others persecute you,
help them in all possible ways.
You will attain immense strength.
You will control anger and pride.
You will enjoy peace, poise and serenity.
You will become divine.

— *Swami Sivanada*

SCRIPTURAL READINGS

Consider your call, my dear people; not many of you were wise according to worldly standards, not many were powerful, not many were of noble birth; but God chose what is foolish in the world to shame the wise, God chose what is weak in the world to shame the strong, God chose what is low and despised in the world, even things that are not, to bring to nothing things that are, so that no human being might boast in the presence of God. God is the source of your life in Christ Jesus, whom God made our wisdom, our righteousness and sanctification and redemption; therefore, as it is written, "Let those who boast, boast of Christ."

I Corinthians 1:26-31

"May Christ dwell in your hearts through faith, and may charity be the root and foundation of your life. Then may you grasp fully, with all the saints, the breadth and length and height and depth of Christ's love, and experience this love which surpasses all knowledge, so that you may attain to the very fullness of God."

Ephesians 3:17-19

At that time Jesus said, "You are the salt of the earth; but if salt has lost its taste, how shall its saltness be restored? It is no longer good for anything except to be thrown out and trodden underfoot.

"You are the light of the world. A city set on a hill cannot be hid. Nor do people light a lamp and put it under a bushel, but on a stand, and it gives light to all in the house. Let your light so shine before others, that they may see your good works and give glory to your God who is in heaven."

Matthew 5:13-16

Thus says God:
I will lead her into the desert
and speak to her heart.
She shall respond there as in the days of her
youth,
when she came up from the land of Egypt.
I will espouse you to me forever:
I will espouse you in right and in justice,
in love and in mercy;
I will espouse you in fidelity,
and you shall know God.

Hosea 2:16, 17, 21-22

When the spirit from on high is poured out on us, then will the desert become an orchard, and the orchard be regarded as a forest. Right will dwell in the desert and justice abide in the orchard. Justice will bring about peace; right will produce calm and security. My people will live in peaceful country, in secure dwellings and quiet resting places.

Isaiah 32:15-20

You rich, weep and wail over your impending miseries. Your wealth has rotted, your fine wardrobe has grown moth-eaten, your gold and silver have corroded, and their corrosion shall be a testimony against you; it will devour your flesh like a fire. See what you have stored up for yourselves against the last days. Here, crying aloud, are the wages you withheld from the farmhands who harvested your fields. The shouts of the harvesters have reached the ears of the God of hosts. You live in wanton luxury on the earth; you fattened yourselves for the day of slaughter. You condemned, even killed, the just ones; they do not resist you.

James 5:1-6

Peace is my parting gift to you, my own peace, such as the world cannot give. Set your troubled hearts at rest and banish your fears.

John 14:27

Your heart is full of mercy, O God. The bright dawn will break upon us, giving light to those in darkness, guiding hearts to the way of peace.

Luke 1:78-79

My brothers and sisters, remember that you have been called to live in freedom — but not a freedom that gives free rein to the flesh. Out of love, place yourselves at one another's service. The whole law has found its fulfillment in this one saying: "You shall love your neighbor as yourself." If you go on biting and tearing one another to pieces, take care! You will end up in mutual destruction.

Galatians 5:13-15

Thus says God:
"Share your bread with the hungry,
  and bring the homeless poor into your house;
when you see the naked, cover them,
  and do not hide yourselves from your own
  flesh.
Then shall your light break forth like the dawn,
  and your healing shall spring up speedily;
your righteousness shall go before you,
  the glory of God shall be your rear guard.
Then you shall call, and God will answer;
  you shall cry, and God will say, Here I am.
If you take away from the midst of you the yoke,
  the pointing of the finger, and speaking
  wickedness,
if you pour yourselves out for the hungry
  and satisfy the desire of the afflicted,
then shall your light rise in the darkness
  and your gloom be as the noonday."

Isaiah 58:7-10

But the wisdom from above is pure, first of
all; it is also peaceful, gentle, and friendly; it is
full of compassion and produces a harvest of
good deeds; it is free from prejudice and hypocrisy.

James 3:17

God will wipe away every tear from their eyes, and death shall be no more, neither shall there be mourning nor crying nor pain any more, for the former things have passed away. And the One who sat on the throne said, "Behold, I make all things new."

Revelation 21:4-5

Say to those whose hearts are frightened:
    Be strong, fear not!
Here is your God
    who comes with vindication;
With divine recompense
    God comes to save you.
Then will the eyes of the blind be opened,
    the ears of the deaf be cleared;
Then will the lame leap like a stag,
    then the tongue of the dumb will sing.
Streams will burst forth in the desert,
    and rivers in the steppe.
The burning sands will become pools,
    and the thirsty ground, springs of water.

Isaiah 35:4-7

Come to me, all you who labor and are heavy
laden, and I will give you rest. Take my yoke
upon you, and learn from me; for I am gentle and
lowly in heart, and you will find rest for your
souls. For my yoke is easy, and my burden is
light.

Matthew 11:29-30

Wolves and sheep will live together in peace,
and leopards will lie down with young goats.
Calves and lion cubs will feed together,
and little children will take care of them.
Cows and bears will eat together,
and their calves and cubs will lie down in peace.
Lions will eat straw as cattle do.
Even a baby will not be harmed
if it plays near a poisonous snake.
On Zion, God's holy hill, there will be nothing
harmful or evil. The land will be as full of
knowledge of the Lord as the seas are full of
water.

Isaiah 11:6-9

Because you are God's chosen ones, holy and beloved, clothe yourselves with heartfelt mercy, with kindness, humility, meekness, and patience. Bear with one another; forgive whatever grievances you have against one another. Forgive as God has forgiven you. Over all these virtues put on love, which binds the rest together and makes them perfect. Christ's peace must reign in your hearts, since as members of the one body you have been called to that peace.

Colossians 3:12-15

Who shall separate us from the love of Christ? Shall tribulation, or distress, or persecution, or famine, or nakedness, or peril, or sword?

No, in all these things we are more than conquerors through the one who loved us. For I am sure that neither death, nor life, nor angels, nor principalities, nor things present, nor things to come, nor powers, nor height, nor depth, nor anything else in all creation, will be able to separate us from the love of God in Christ Jesus our Lord.

Romans 8:35, 37-39

Have no anxiety about anything; but in everything by prayer and supplication with thanksgiving let your requests be known to God. And the peace of God, which passes all understanding, will keep your hearts and your minds in Christ Jesus.

Finally, my dear people, whatever is true, whatever is honorable, whatever is just, whatever is pure, whatever is lovely, whatever is gracious, if there is any excellence, if there is anything worthy of praise, think about these things. What you have learned and received and heard and seen in me, do; and the God of peace will be with you.

Philippians 4:6-9

What is good has been explained to you; this is what Yahweh asks of you, only this: to act justly, to love tenderly and to walk humbly with your God.

Micah 6:8

Rising early the next morning, Jesus went off to a lonely place in the desert; there he was absorbed in prayer.

Mark 1:35

God who said, "Let light shine out of darkness," has shone in our hearts, that we in turn might make known the glory of God shining on the face of Christ. This treasure we possess in earthen vessels to make it clear that its surpassing power comes from God and not from us. We are afflicted in every way possible, but we are not crushed; full of doubts, we never despair. We are persecuted but never abandoned; we are struck down but never destroyed. Continually we carry about in our bodies the dying of Jesus so that in our bodies the life of Jesus may also be revealed. While we live we are constantly being delivered to death for Jesus' sake, so that the life of Jesus may be revealed in our mortal flesh.

2 Corinthians 4:6-11

To you who hear me, I say: Love your enemies, do good to those who hate you; bless those who curse you; and pray for those who maltreat you. When someone slaps you on one cheek, turn the other. . . . Be compassionate, as your God is compassionate.

Luke 6:27-29

And I will give them one heart, and put a new spirit within them; I will take the stony heart out of their bodies and give them a heart of flesh, that they may walk in my statutes and keep my ordinances and obey them, and they shall be my people and I will be their God.

Ezechiel 11:19-21

Jesus came to Nazareth where he had been reared, and entering the synagogue on the sabbath as he was in the habit of doing, he stood up to do the reading. When the book of the prophet Isaiah was handed him, he unrolled the scroll and found the passage where it was written: "The spirit of God is upon me; therefore God has anointed me. God has sent me to bring glad tidings to the poor, to proclaim liberty to captives, recovery of sight to the blind and release to prisoners, to announce a year of favor from our God."

Rolling up the scroll he gave it back to the assistant and sat down. Everyone in the synagogue had their eyes fixed on him. Then he began by saying "Today this Scripture passage is fulfilled in your hearing."

Luke 4:16-21

"Arise, my beloved, my beautiful one,
    and come!
For see, the winter is past,
    the rains are over and gone.
The flowers appear on the earth,
    the time of pruning the vines has come,
    and the song of the dove is heard
        in our land.
The fig tree puts forth it figs,
    and the vines, in bloom, give forth fragrance.
Arise, my beloved, my beautiful one,
    and come!
O my dove in the clefts of the rock,
    in the secret recesses of the cliff,
Let me see you,
    let me hear your voice,
For your voice is sweet,
    and you are lovely."

        Song of Songs 2:10b-14

Everyone who thirsts,
    come to the waters;
and whoever has no money,
    come, buy and eat!
Come, buy wine and milk
    without money and without price.
Why do you spend your money for that which
    is not bread,
    and your labor for that which does not
    satisfy?
Hearken diligently to me, and eat what is good,
    and delight yourselves in fatness.
Incline your ear, and come to me;
    hear, that your soul may live;
and I will make with you an everlasting cove-
    nant,
    my steadfast, sure love for David.
    Isaiah 55:1-3

If I speak with human tongues and angelic
as well, but do not have love, I am a noisy gong,
a clanging symbol. If I have the gift of prophecy
and, with full knowledge, comprehend all mysteries, if I have faith great enough to move
mountains, but have not love, I am nothing. If I
give everything I have to feed the poor and hand
over my body to be burned, but have not love, I
gain nothing.

Love is patient; love is kind. Love is not jealous, it does not put on airs, it is not snobbish. Love is never rude, it is not self-seeking, it is not prone to anger; neither does it brood over injuries. Love does not rejoice in what is wrong but rejoices with the truth. There is no limit to love's forbearance, to its trust, its hope, its power to endure.

Love never fails.

I Corinthians 13:1-8

My brothers and sisters, your faith in our Lord Jesus Christ glorified must not allow of favoritism. Suppose there should come into your assembly a man fashionably dressed, with gold rings on his fingers, and at the same time a poor man dressed in shabby clothes. Suppose further you were to take notice of the well-dressed man and say, "Sit over here, please"; whereas you were to say to the poor man, "You can stand!" or "Sit over there by my footrest." Have you not in a case like this discriminated in your hearts? Have you not set yourselves up as judges who hand down corrupt decisions?

Listen, dear brothers and sisters. Did not God choose those who are poor in the eyes of the world to be rich in faith and heirs of the kingdom promised to those who love God?

James 2:1-5

Pass no judgment, and you will not be judged; do not condemn, and you will not be condemned; acquit, and you will be acquitted; give, and gifts will be given you. Good measure, pressed down, shaken together, and running over, will be poured into your lap; for whatever measure you deal out to others will be dealt to you in return.

Luke 6:37-38

Can a mother forget her infant,
be without tenderness for the child
   of her womb?
Even should she forget,
I will never forget you.
See, upon the palms of my hands I have
written your name.

Isaiah 49:15-16

     Jesus summoned the crowd with his disciples and said to them: "If you wish to come after me, you must deny your very self, take up your cross, and follow in my steps."

Mark 8:34

If you shut your ear to the cry of the poor
You yourself will call and not be heard.

Proverbs 21:13

Love bears all things, believes all things,
hopes all things, endures all things.
> *I Corinthians 13:6*

"You, O human one, I have made a sentry for the
house of Israel; whenever you hear a word from
my mouth, you shall give them warning from me.
If I say to the wicked, O wicked ones, you shall
surely die, and you do not speak to warn the
wicked to turn from their way, those wicked ones
shall die in their iniquity, but their blood I will
require at your hand. But if you warn the
wicked to turn from their way, and they do not
turn from their way, they shall die in their
iniquity, but you will have saved your life."
> *Ezekiel 33:7-9*

If you oppress poor people, you insult the
God who makes them; but kindness shown to the
poor is an act of worship.
> *Proverbs 14:31*

"Speak up for people who cannot speak for
themselves. Protect the rights of all who are
helpless. Speak for them and be a righteous
judge. Protect the rights of the poor and needy."
> *Book of Proverbs 31:8-9*

"I have come to set the earth on fire, and how I wish it were already blazing! There is a baptism with which I must be baptized, and how great is my anguish until it is accomplished!"

Luke 12:49-50

One of the scribes asked Jesus, "Which is the first of all the commandments?" Jesus replied, "The first is this: 'Hear, O Israel! God is God alone! You shall love God with all your heart, with all your soul, with all your mind, and with all your strength.' The second is this: 'You shall love your neighbor as yourself.' There is no other commandment greater than these."

Mark 12:28-30

"The group of believers was one in heart and mind. No one said that any of their belongings were their own, but they all shared with one another everything they had. With great power the apostles gave witness to the resurrection of Jesus, and God poured rich blessings on them all. There was no one in the group who was in need. Those who owned fields or houses would sell them, bring the money received from the sale, and turn it over to the apostles; and the money was distributed to each one according to their need."

Acts 4:32-35

O the depth of the riches and wisdom and knowledge of God! How unsearchable are God's judgments and how inscrutable God's ways!
"For who has known the mind of God,
or who has been God's counselor?"
"Or who has given a gift to God
that would require repayment?"
For from God and through God and to God are all things, to whom be glory forever. Amen.

Romans 11:33-36

I prayed, and prudence was given me;
I pleaded, and the spirit of Wisdom came to me.
I preferred her to scepter and throne,
And deemed riches nothing in comparison with her,
nor did I liken any priceless gem to her;
Because all gold, in view of her, is a little sand,
and before her, silver is to be accounted mire.
Beyond health and comeliness I loved her,
And I chose to have her rather than the light,
because the splendor of her never yields to sleep.
Yet all good things together came to me in her company,
and countless riches at her hands.

Wisdom 7:7-11

A parable Jesus put before them, saying, "The dominion of heaven is like treasure hidden in a field, which someone found and covered up; then in her joy she goes and sells all that she has and buys that field.

"Again, the dominion of heaven is like a merchant in search of fine pearls, who, on finding one pearl of great value, went and sold all that he had and bought it."

Matthew 13:44-46

And seeing the multitudes, he went up into a mountain: and when he was set, his disciples came to him and he opened his mouth, and taught them, saying, "Blessed are the poor in spirit: for theirs is the reign of heaven. Blessed are they that mourn: for they shall be comforted. Blessed are the meek: for they shall inherit the earth. Blessed are they who hunger and thirst after righteousness: for they shall be filled. Blessed are the merciful: for they shall obtain mercy. Blessed are the pure in heart: for they shall see God. Blessed are the peacemakers: for they shall be called the children of God. Blessed are they who are persecuted for righteousness' sake: for theirs is the reign of heaven. Blessed are you, when others shall revile you, and persecute you, and say all manner of evil against you falsely, for my sake. Rejoice, and be exceedingly glad: for great is your reward in heaven: for so were the prophets before you persecuted.

Luke 6:20-23

The Spirit helps us in our weakness; for we do not know how to pray as we ought, but that very Spirit intercedes for us with signs too deep for words. And the one who searches human hearts knows what is the mind of the Spirit, because the Spirit intercedes for the saints according to the will of God.

Romans 8:26-27

God's word is living and effective, sharper than any two edged sword. It penetrates and divides soul and spirit, joints and marrow; it judges the reflections and thoughts of the heart. Nothing is concealed from God; all lies bare and exposed to the eyes of God to whom we must render an account.

Hebrews 4:12-13

Though Christ was in the form of God, he did not deem equality with God something to be grasped at. Rather, Christ emptied himself and took the form of a servant, being born in our likeness. Christ was known to be of human estate, and it was thus that he humbled himself, obediently accepting even death, death on a cross! Because of this, God highly exalted Christ and bestowed on him the name above every other name, so that at the name of Jesus every knee must bend in the heavens, on the earth, and under the earth, and every tongue proclaim to the glory of God: Jesus Christ is Savior!

Philippians 2:6-11

Acknowledgments

Permission to reprint the following passages in *The Fire of Peace* is gratefully acknowledged:

p. 4, Dom Helder Camara; p. 5. Robert Drinan, SJ; p.9, Marcia Falk; p. 251, Lololomai; p. 252, Jim Wallis; p. 253, Thomas Merton and St. Augustine of Hippo; p. 261, Rabbi Bunan from *Peace Prayers,* copyright © 1992, HarperCollins Publishers, 10 East 53rd Street, New York, NY 10022.

p. 6, "For Calm" from *Guerrillas of Grace,* by Ted Loder, © 1984, Lura Media Inc., San Diego, California.

p. 27, "For Political Prisoners," adapted from a text from Amnesty International, 1 Easton St., London WC1X 8DJ.

p. 33, "For Racial Harmony," Christian Aid, 240-250 Ferndale Road, London SW9 8BH.

p. 36, "For the United States" by Leslie Brandt, Concordia Publishing House, 3558 South Jefferson Ave., St. Louis, MO 63118.

p. 39, "For the Human Family," *Christopher Prayers for Today,* 1972, The Christophers, 12 East 48th St., New York, NY 10017.

p. 42, "For the Work of Our Hands," Diann Neu, WATER, Silver Spring, MD.

p. 50, "For the Earth's Blessings" (For the Ecology), Synapses, 1821 West Cullerton, Chicago, IL 60608.

p. 145, "Prayer to Mary for the Sick," from *Prayer for Each Day*, Editions du Centurion, 17 rue de Babylone, Paris 7E, France.

p. 173, "Litany for Peace" from Catholic Peace Action, 7 Putney Bridge Road, London SW18 1HX.

p. 178, "Little Litany of Praise" by Blanche Jennings Thompson, Novalis, 6255 Hutchison St., Suite 103, Montreal, Quebec H2V 4C7, Canada.

p. 195, "Creed for a Nuclear Age," Council of Churches for Britain and Ireland, 35 - 41 Lower Marsh, London SEI 7RL.

p. 218 "Prayer for Fasting"; p. 257, Balthasar Fischer from *Easter*, Archdiocese of Chicago, Office of Peace and Justice, and Office of Liturgy, 155 East Superior Ave., Chicago, IL 60611.

p. 229, "Reflections on Becoming an Instrument of Peace," *The Franciscan*, 1981, Hillfield, Dorchester, Dorset.

p. 244, *Letters to Contemplatives*, by William Johnston, Orbis Books, 1991, Maryknoll, NY 10545.

MEMBERSHIP APPLICATION

Membership in Pax Christi USA is by direct application to the national office only.

I support the purpose of Pax Christi USA and wish to become a member. Standard membership fee is $20 a year.

Enclosed is my membership of

____$35 ____$20 ____$50 ____$100 ____other

____ At this time I cannot contribute the full $20, but I wish to be a member of Pax Christi USA. Enclosed is $_____

____ I would like to join a local group.

____ I would like to organize a local Pax Christi group.

____ Please send me information on making a bequest.

Name _____

Address _____

City _____

State _____ Zip _____

Phone _____

Send to Pax Christi USA, 532 West Eighth Street, Erie, PA 16502 814/453-4955.

STATEMENT OF PURPOSE

Pax Christi USA intends to contribute to building peace and justice by exploring and articulating the ideal of Christian nonviolence and by striving to apply it to personal life and to the structures of society. Pax Christi USA invites concerned Catholics to respond to the Church's call to evaluate war with an entirely new attitude and to take an active role in making secure a peace based on justice and love.

As a section of Pax Christi International, Pax Christi USA seeks, with the help of its episcopal members, to establish peacemaking as a priority for the United States Catholic Church. To accomplish this, Pax Christi USA works with various Catholic communities and agencies, and also collaborates with other groups committed to nonviolent peacemaking.

Pax Christi USA finds its strength in the efforts of committed individuals to follow the gospel imperative of peacemaking...an imperative repeated throughout the Christian tradition, most recently by Pope John Paul II: "Peace is our work...To everyone, Christians, believers, and men and women of good will, I say: Do not be afraid to take a chance on peace, to teach peace...Peace will be our last word of history."